Ooh Lala

Delicious Punjabi Food, Simplified

LALA RUKH

50 Delicious and Easy-to-master Pakistani-American Recipes and Enchanting Stories

To know about a country's cuisine is to better know the customs and the richness or poverty of a place, and the spirit of those who inhabit it. It is, above all, to participate in the symbolic celebration of the shared past.

~ GINETTE OLIVESI-LORENZI

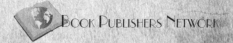
BOOK PUBLISHERS NETWORK

Book Publishers Network
P.O. Box 2256
Bothell, WA 98041
425-483-3040
www.bookpublishersnetwork.com

10 9 8 7 6 5 4 3 2 1

Printed in the United States of America

LCCN: 2013953057
ISBN: 978-1-940598-13-0

Editor: Julie Scandora
Indexer: Carolyn Acheson
Book Design: Laura Zugzda
Food Photos: Lala Rukh & Eli Simmonds

Dedication

I DEDICATE THIS BOOK

TO IJAZ,

MY HUSBAND AND TEACHER

IN LIFE

Table of Contents

Lala, seventeen years old, Lahore, Pakistan

Lala and husband, Ijaz, Charleston, South Carolina, 1984

Lala and daughter Ann, Birmingham, England, 1975

Introduction

As a child in Pakistan, I learned to appreciate seasonal and healthy foods. My mother provided hearty staples, like parathas and fried eggs, rice with dal, goat and pea curry, and the occasional tasty delicacy, like samosas with tamarind chutney, to feed her large family. She did not insist we help with cooking. I did not have time to cook, yet somehow my world was centered in the kitchen. My childhood memories, sweet and bitter, are tinged with the aroma of cardamom-infused *chai*, the soft silkiness of freshly made butter on warm flatbread, and the cool sweetness of yogurt *lassi* on balmy, summer nights. Outside, we swung from the mango trees, snacked on guavas picked from the branch, and helped Ami Jan by gathering fresh carrots and radishes from the garden. At the end of the day, at my father's insistence, we always enjoyed a family meal, gathered around a table or sheet, laughing and arguing in turn, and of course, feasting on fresh, simple food.

During graduate school, I met my husband (also my teacher, but that is another book). We were soon blessed by a beautiful child, our first daughter, Ann. When Ann was still a baby, we moved to Birmingham, England, where my husband, Ijaz, was studying for his PhD in endocrinology. As with many young wives, I was on my own, away from my mother and aunts, and then, I first started preparing meals for my small family. And while I had grown up with delicious and aromatic foods, my cooking skills took some trial and error to develop, as my patient husband can attest. At the time, I was teaching biology at Highgate High School in Birmingham, England. I tried to learn more about cooking from everyone I encountered.

My Indian-British students taught me their techniques for preparing fresh *parathas*. By observing the cook at our local fish-and-chips place, I learned how to batter and fry perfectly tender fillets of fish. In my classes, I enjoyed talking about Pakistani culture, especially the cuisine. It became a tool for motivating my students to develop their understanding of nutrition and their bodies. My students would share their culinary adventures, and a lively dialog and cultural exchange would follow.

By the time we moved to the U.S., Ann's darling little sister, Arooj, had joined us. I kept busy as a wife, mother, and high school science teacher. Still, even with this busy schedule, I felt it was important to prepare fresh meals for my family. Given my childhood experiences and background in the life sciences, I gravitated toward fresh, organic foods. I learned to prep ahead of time, and most Sundays, I cooked a week's worth of food.

For almost two decades while we lived in Port Orange and I taught at Spruce Creek High School in Port Orange Florida, Ijaz would visit the local farmers' market on Saturday. When the girls were little, sometimes I would mind the girls while he went. Other times, he would take the girls so I could study or write my lesson plans. Each time, he brought home fresh fruits and vegetables, treasures we would all enjoy through the next week. On Sunday, we would prepare a brunch with fruit chat (page 12), omelet (page 62), and scones with hot green tea. It became a ritual Arooj and Ann looked forward to through their growing years.

Over time, my appreciation and love for preparing fresh, elegant, and simple meals grew. I learned more about different culinary traditions, but still my heart belongs to the foods of Pakistan. I miss the rich, aromatic flavors of my childhood in Pakistan, not just the food, but also the people and landscape. I want to share with you Pakistan's beauty and the spirit of the people who call it home.

This is a time of turmoil for Pakistan. Despite their hardships,

the people of this vibrant country do not lose their sense of humor, generosity, and appreciation for life. From the poor who are living crammed in mud huts to the rich in their mansions with rolling lawns, Pakistani people are proud of their heritage. It is my wish not only to share simple Pakistani recipes but also to help educate my western readers about one of the oldest cultures on earth and to share the spirit of a country that will always be close to my heart.

In Pakistan, cooking often carries a social stigma. It is felt that cooking is only for the lower classes, the *khansama* or *bawarchi*. I say cooking is for everyone. We should all be so lucky to call ourselves a khansama. What better way to connect with the people around you, to show your love, than with a warm dish of something that fills the stomach and soul.

My cooking is a fusion of American, British, and Pakistani ingredients and methods. It is Pakistani with a twist. Typical Pakistani food has more *ghee* and spices and is much more time intensive. My cooking is simpler, requires less prep time, and utilizes fewer ingredients. These are dishes I made for my family even when teaching six periods a day and studying for a master's degree. A busy lifestyle and two small daughters encouraged me to find healthy shortcuts for my favorite foods. Over the years, I started altering fattening recipes to be healthier. For example, using vegetable or olive oil instead of ghee, using milder peppers to lessen the heat, and not overloading with spices are some ways I have changed recipes.

All of the dishes throughout the book are designed to feed six to eight people. Even if your family is small, keep some in the fridge for later or invite some friends over to share.

A few years ago, Ijaz was diagnosed with celiac sprue. We found out that he cannot eat gluten, a substance found in wheat, oat, and other grains. **Many of the dishes in this book are gluten free and I have marked them with an asterisk.**

Most of the dishes except fish and meat recipes are vegetarian.

I do not hesitate to use modern kitchen gadgets, like a food processor, slow cooker, and rice cooker. Sometimes my Pakistani/American friends complain about the tedious and time-consuming methods of our cooking, or American friends say they love Pakistani/Indian food but are too intimidated to try cooking it themselves. My dishes save time but lose no taste or nutrients. These recipes make Pakistani cooking enjoyable and easier to prepare so that I can spend less time in tedious preparations and more time in sharing my food and culture with family and friends.

Even a beginner cook, or people who do not have much time to spare, can enjoy the many flavors of Pakistan with my simple recipes. I have an easy-going cooking philosophy. You do not have to be perfect. Preparing food for your family is about having fun and loving what you are doing. If you mess up, maybe you have learned or created something new. Serendipity! Enjoy your creation or throw it on the compost pile and start something new.

I see this book as something of a political act, trying to create awareness about a unique culture, one recipe at a time.

About the Spices

To make tasty dishes with distinctive flavors of various spices, you will need some basic spices, four whole spices for rice and four ground spices for curries. As these spices do not spoil easily, I buy them in bulk. I fill small containers for everyday cooking and save the extra in airtight containers in the refrigerator. This leaves me all set when I am ready to create!

Whole Spices

Black or green
     cardamom seeds
Cinnamon sticks
Cloves
Cumin seeds

Ground Spices

Coriander
Cumin, white or black
Hot red pepper, cayenne,
     Indian pepper or any
     other hot variety
Turmeric

You may keep coriander and cumin whole and grind using a pestle and mortar or an electric coffee grinder while you are preparing food. It will give your food a better flavor and taste.

To roast cumin seeds, add the desired amount to a hot skillet and cook on medium heat for a few minutes. It releases the oils to give it a stronger flavor.

I also suggest keeping the following spices and spice mixtures for use in special dishes:

Chat masala
Fennel seeds
Mango powder
Pomegranate powder or seeds
Tamarind paste

For garnish, I use fresh cilantro, mint, or ginger. Like most herbs and spices, the spices used in my cooking not only add flavor and taste but also have health benefits, which you can easily learn about from many books or on the Internet. And, of course, no curry is complete without a sprinkle of garam masala.

GARAM MASALA

This is my mother's recipe.

Ingredients

¼ cup whole cloves
½ cup black peppercorns
7 medium-sized cinnamon sticks
1½ cups cumin seeds
½ cup coriander seeds
½ cup whole black cardamom

Procedure

1. Grind cloves and peppercorns in a food processor. Set aside. In the same container, grind cinnamon sticks.

2. In a heavy-bottom skillet over low to medium heat, roast cumin and coriander seeds together for 5 minutes. Let cool.

3. Grind roasted cumin and coriander seeds to a powder.

4. Remove seeds from the cardamoms. Grind seeds to a powder.

5. Mix all spices together.

6. Keep in an airtight container. It will last up to 6 months.

Tip: Sprinkle about ½ teaspoon on curry dishes when ready to serve. Or place in small bowls for individual servings on the side.

Appetizers

Eggplant or Spinach Pakoras*

Samosa with Tamarind Chutney

Aaloo Kabobs (Potato Patties)

Fruit Chat with Fresh Sweet-and-sour Dressing*

Shrimp Kabobs

* Gluten free

EGGPLANT OR SPINACH PAKORAS*

Ingredients

1 small eggplant, 1-2 inches in diameter, or $1/8$ pound (about 15)
   healthy, medium-size spinach leaves

2–4 tablespoons lemon juice

1 cup gram flour

½ teaspoon baking soda

1 teaspoon salt

2 teaspoons cayenne

3 teaspoons ground coriander

1 teaspoon roasted cumin seeds

½ cup water

1 cup oil

Procedure

1. Cut the eggplant into slices $1/8$-inch-thick. Wet both sides with lemon juice. Set aside. Or, if using spinach leaves, wash and dry each leaf.

2. In a bowl, mix gram flour (also known as *besan*, available at Asian or Middle Eastern food stores), baking soda, salt, cayenne, coriander, cumin seeds, and water. Mixture should have the consistency of pancake batter. Set aside.

3. In a large skillet, heat oil over medium heat. Oil should cover the bottom of the pan completely and be approximately 1 inch in depth. Test if oil is hot enough by dropping ½ teaspoon of batter into it; if batter sizzles, oil is at appropriate temperature.

4. Dip two to three pieces of eggplant or spinach leaves, depending on what type of pakoras you are making, into the gram-flour mixture. Be sure to coat both sides of eggplant or spinach well. Gently place into hot oil and fry both sides until coating appears golden brown. Remove from oil and place on paper towel to absorb excess oil. Repeat.

Tip: Tastes great with salsa, mint chutney, or just ketchup. Use as a stuffing for various kinds of wraps.

SAMOSA WITH TAMARIND CHUTNEY

Ingredients

2 medium potatoes, washed and peeled

¼ cup finely chopped fresh coriander leaves

1 teaspoon roasted cumin seeds

2 teaspoons red pepper

4 teaspoons ground coriander

1 teaspoon salt

4 large egg-roll wrappers (found in the grocery section of most
supermarkets)

1 egg white, well beaten

2 cups vegetable oil

½ cup water

Tamarind chutney (see page 20)

Procedure

1. **To make potato mixture**: Cut potatoes into halves and boil
    in a medium-sized pan of water. Remove from pan when
    fork tender. Cool until able to handle comfortably with
    hands. Mash potatoes until they are the consistency of very
    lumpy mashed potatoes. Add coriander leaves and spices to
    potatoes. Mix well and set aside. Mixture should remain
    lumpy!

2. **To form samosas**: Cut each large egg-roll wrapper into four
    equal-sized squares. Very thinly spread egg white around
    the perimeter of each square (about ½-inch wide). Place
    approximately 1 teaspoon of the potato mixture on each
    square. Fold square into a triangle. Press edges with a fork
    (as you would with piecrust).

3. **Frying samosas**: In a medium-sized frying pan, heat vegetable oil. After about 2–3 minutes, drop in a piece of egg-roll wrapper to check if the oil is hot enough.
   If the egg-roll wrapper turns crispy right away, your oil is hot enough. Add 2–4 samosas at a time to the oil. Cook both sides until the egg-roll wrapper turns light brown. Remove samosas and place on 3–4 layers of paper towels to absorb excess oil. Repeat the process.

4. Serve hot with tamarind chutney (see page 20).

Tip: Also tastes great with mint chutney. If you have the time or energy to make your own samosa dough, please do so (and invite me over)! Egg-roll wrappers are a tasty alternative for the busier cook.

AALOO KABOBS (POTATO PATTIES)

Ingredients

2 pounds potatoes (preferably small red)

½ cup scallions, washed and finely chopped

½ cup coriander leaves, washed and chopped

2–4 teaspoons ground red pepper

1 teaspoon ground mango powder (*amchoor*) or lemon juice

4 teaspoons ground coriander

½ cup bread or cracker crumbs

1–2 teaspoons salt

1 cup vegetable or any other oil

1 egg, well beaten

Procedure

1. Wash the potatoes. Add 4 cups water and boil the potatoes for 15–20 minutes or till able to pierce with a fork.

2. Remove from heat. Wash potatoes in cold water and remove peel. Use potato masher to mash the potatoes.

3. Add all remaining ingredients, except egg and oil.

4. Take out golf-ball-sized chunks and flatten them into roughly ½-inch-thick patties. Set the patties aside.

5. In a heavy-bottom frying pan, heat ½ cup of oil over medium heat. Take one patty at a time, dip it into egg, and gently lower into hot oil. Cook 4–5 kabobs at a time, flipping a few times until both sides are golden brown. Place them on paper towels to absorb excess oil. Add and heat more oil if needed.

6. Serve warm with mint, mango, or tamarind chutney.

Tip: Potato patties can be prepared 2–3 days in advance and kept in the refrigerator. Fry before serving.

FRUIT CHAT WITH FRESH SWEET-AND-SOUR DRESSING*

Makes 8 servings

Ingredients

2 oranges
½ lemon,
1 teaspoon salt
1 teaspoon cayenne
1 teaspoon mango powder (see note below)
4 teaspoons brown sugar
½ cup cantaloupe, peeled and cut into bite-size pieces
1 banana, peeled and cut into bite-size pieces
1 pear, peeled and cut into bite-size pieces
1 apple, peeled and cut into bite-size pieces
8–10 strawberries, halved
8–10 seedless grapes
½ cup raisins

Procedure

1. **For dressing:** Squeeze juice of oranges and lemon into a cup. Stir in salt, cayenne, mango powder, and sugar.
2. **For chat:** In glass bowl, pour dressing over cantaloupe, banana, pear, apple, halved strawberries, grapes, and raisins. Mix thoroughly without breaking the fruit pieces. Serve immediately.

Note: Mango powder is frequently used instead of tamarind, the other important sour element in Pakistani-Indian cuisine. Mango powder is much weaker than tamarind and has a subtle sour taste. It is used for a hint of tartness or when the dark color of tamarind is not wanted.

Tip: Dressing and chat can be prepared several hours in advance and stored separately in the refrigerator. Mix together just before serving.

SHRIMP KABOBS

Ingredients

1 pound shrimp, deveined, peeled, and chopped in a food
processor (it should be much coarser than the texture of
ground beef)

½ cup scallions, washed and finely diced

½ cup coriander leaves, washed and finely chopped

1 tablespoon crushed ginger

½ cup crushed crackers or breadcrumbs

3 teaspoons ground coriander

2 teaspoons ground red pepper

1–2 teaspoons salt

½ cup oil

1 egg, well beaten

Procedure

1. Mix all ingredients except oil and egg.

2. Take out golf-ball-sized chunks and flatten them into roughly ½-inch-thick patties. Set patties aside.

3. In a heavy-bottom frying pan, add half the oil and heat over medium heat. Take one patty at a time, dip it into egg, and gently lower into hot oil. Cook 4–5 kabobs at a time, flipping a few times until both sides are golden brown. Place them on paper towels to absorb excess oil.

4. Serve warm with mint, mango, or tamarind chutney.

Tip: These kabobs can also be used as filling for sandwiches or with a lovely, fresh green salad.

EARLY MORNING PICK
Summer 1963

I woke up one summer dawn at Aba Ji's house, as I often did. My favorite thing about Aba Ji and Bi Ji's house were the green gardens and trees, including pomegranate, guava, banana, date, every tree you might have found in Eden.

The early morning dew clung to my brow and fingertips. Black curls pressed to my forehead. I wiped them back and gently pressed my palm to the delicate mosquito net, the one Ami Jan had sewn and had propped over our beds so that we could sleep undisturbed by the insects that flew through the night air. I eased out of my cot, careful not to disturb my sleeping brothers. I pulled the net over my head and tucked it back underneath the beds. I glanced at the rising and falling chests of my brothers and tiptoed towards my beloved mango trees. The grass was wet and cool under my feet, and the world was awash in the gauzy pinks and oranges of a new day. When I reached the front yard, I sprawled out on the stairs overlooking the mango trees. There were four of them, stretched up proud from the grass, showing off their broad waxy leaves and dangling yellow and green fruit. If I fixed my eyes just so, the trees became the great and tall centurions of God, come to present me with tributes of precious stones. The ground bubbled with the fallen baubles, too many for the trees to hold. Large, juicy golden orbs speckled with jewels of green, yellow, and pink.

In the silence of dawn, before there were other children clamoring about, the treasure belonged only to me. My mouth watered at the thought of the sweet, juicy mango flesh. My eyes moved over the ground from one ripened treasure to the next. I pulled myself up, tall and straight like a queen about to deliver a proclamation to her subjects. I stepped into the yard and began to gather the fruits from

the ground. The gauzy cotton of my kamiz trailed in the wet morning grass. The mango skins felt smooth and cool against my arms, like rocks just pulled from the river. I filled my arms with as many mangoes as I could hold, and soon I had made a small mound of them under one of the trees.

I surveyed my coffer. When the other children awoke, they would want to share my riches, so I hid the best one for myself in a little space on the other side of the tree. I was the queen of the kingdom, after all. I stretched out luxuriously next to my bounty, running my fingers over the dewy blades of grass, which felt like soft whiskers poking up from the earth. I lay there, in the quiet of the morning, before there were brothers and sister and cousins to look after, before there were busy adults clucking and shooing and working around the house. I looked up at the pink and orange sky filtered through the mango leaves and imagined my kingdom, a lavish palace, a beautiful princess riding a tiger, caves filled with mountains of treasure. Before anyone else woke up, it was all mine.

Soon I could hear the stirrings of life from within the house and my brothers in the backyard. Ami Jan had already come out and chuckled at the sight of me, splayed out next to a pile of ripe mangoes. "Well," she said, "I guess I know what you are having for breakfast."

In Pakistan, we do not eat mangoes by cutting; no one would settle for one piece anyway. We gently squeeze the mango, careful not to break it, pull the stem off, and suck the mango out through the hole. That is the way to get the best mango juice. The other children also sat under the trees and sucked on mangoes as the sun rose higher in the sky and the air grew warmer around us.

Lala, fifteen years old, Lahore, Pakistan

Pickles and Chutneys

Tamarind Chutney*

Mango Chutney*

Mint Chutney*

Samania (Eight-ingredient) Chutney*

Lemon Pickle*

Gluten free

TAMARIND CHUTNEY*

Ingredients

4 teaspoons tamarind paste

1 cup water

2 teaspoons red pepper

1 teaspoon salt

3 teaspoons brown sugar

1 teaspoon cumin seeds

5 mint leaves, finely chopped

Procedure

1. In a small saucepan, mix all ingredients except mint leaves. Cook over low to medium heat until the liquid is reduced to ½ cup, about 10–15 minutes.

2. Let cool. Transfer to a serving dish and garnish with mint leaves.

MANGO CHUTNEY*

Ingredients

½ cup unripe green mango, peeled and diced

1 small hot green pepper, seeds removed

½ teaspoon salt

4 tablespoons plain yogurt

A few sprigs of mint, chopped

Procedure

Grind all ingredients except mint in a blender. Transfer to a serving dish and garnish with mint.

MINT CHUTNEY*

Ingredients

½ cup fresh mint leaves

½ hot green pepper, seeds removed

1 small tomato, seeds removed and
   chopped

2 tablespoons onion, chopped

1 teaspoon salt

4 teaspoons yogurt (be generous)

A few mint leaves for garnish

Procedure

Place all ingredients except mint in a blender. Blend for 30 seconds to 1 minute. Mixture should be slightly finer than salsa in appearance. Garnish with mint leaves.

Tip: Tastes great with pakoras, samosa, fish, or in sandwiches.

SAMANIA (EIGHT-INGREDIENT) CHUTNEY*

My grandmother, Bi Ji's recipe

Ingredients

4 cups green mangoes, peeled and sliced 1–2 inches long and
$1/8$-inch wide (you may use a food processor)

4 cups sugar

2 teaspoons red pepper or more (depending on taste)

1 cup red wine or white or apple cider vinegar

½ cup sultanas (golden raisins)

1 teaspoon black peppercorns

2 teaspoons salt

4–5 cloves garlic, very thinly sliced

2-inch-square piece of ginger, thinly sliced

Procedure

1. Mix sliced mangoes and sugar in a glass dish and leave overnight or for 6–8 hours.

2. Next day, over low to medium heat, cook mixture for 1–2 hours or until the syrup becomes sticky. Do not cover the pot; stir occasionally.

3. Add remaining ingredients and let cook for ½ hour or more if needed. You will be left with a mixture that has a consistency similar to maple syrup. It should be the color of light honey.

4. Your samania is ready. Transfer while still hot to sterilized glass jam jars and seal the lid tightly.

5. Store in the refrigerator. This chutney can last up to a year. Always use a clean spoon to take out the required amount and then save the rest, making sure that the lid is tightly closed.

Tip: An excellent garnish for roasted meat. It can also be used with various appetizers. Always use sparingly.

LEMON PICKLE*

Ingredients

10 fresh lemons, free of brown spots, washed and dried

10 fresh limes, free of brown spots, washed and dried

4 teaspoons salt

2 teaspoons ground red pepper

½ teaspoon kaloniji (Nigella sativa), optional

Procedure

1. Squeeze the lemons, remove seeds, set juice aside.

2. Cut each lime into 4–8 pieces and remove seeds. Do not remove the skin. It becomes softer while the pickle is being aged.

3. In a sterilized glass jar, add lime pieces, lemon juice, salt, and spices.

4. Screw the lid tightly and shake well until all pieces seem to be coated with the lemon juice.

5. Repeat step 4 once a day at least 4 times a week.

6. Achar will be ready in 2–3 weeks.

Tip: Always use dry, clean hands and fork to take the required amount of pickle—1 or 2 slices per person are enough with each meal.

MANGO PICKLING MARATHON
Summer 1963

In high season, the trees were so bountiful we could not eat the ripe mangoes fast enough (and there was also the danger of people stealing the fruit right off the trees). In those times, Aba Ji would hire people to pluck the green fruit from the trees. He would get a big scale, taller than I was, with pans a foot across and a top bar at least a yard long, and measure out baskets of mangoes to give to family and friends, five seers, or about ten pounds, a piece. As he sorted the full baskets, he would smile at me and say, "Families with children get more since sometimes little buchas run off with the best mangoes." The ripe ones from the trees were eaten or given as gifts. Some of the unripe ones were stored in large boxes, stacked between layers of cotton, and locked, of course, to keep out little children.

The next day, Bi Ji and Ami Jan gathered some of the sour mangoes and set up outside on the inner veranda for a long day of pickling and chutney making. It was exciting to think of many mothers and grandmothers and aunts and sisters all over the Punjab, bustling about porches and kitchens pickling their own mangoes. Some families would simply delegate the task to their servants, and others might only be able to make a few jars of pickles. We fell somewhere in-between.

First Ami Jan and Bi Ji carefully washed and dried the mangoes.

"Why do you wash them so much?" I asked my Bi Ji.

"We must get all the dirt off, Bilo."

Bi Ji called me Bilo sometimes because she said I was spry like a little cat ("bili" is a female cat).

"But why do we have to get all the dirt off, Bi Ji?"

"So no fungus or bacteria grows on them in the jar. We must be very careful not even to have dirty hands. Now, Bilo, run and help by shooing away the flies."

I stationed myself nearby, ready to swat away any bugs that might try to get at the pickle. When the women were finished washing all of the fruit, Ami Jan spread the mangoes out to dry on the sheets she and the housekeeper had washed the night before. Bi Ji let me help place a few but only after making sure I had washed my hands.

They had hired some extra help to assist in cutting the mangoes into pieces. They started assembling them into glazed pots. I noticed that some pieces were larger and had skins on them. Those pieces went into big vats. Other pieces were smaller, more delicate. Those pieces went into smaller, prettier pots. One was a shiny robin's egg blue with a beautiful gold print.

"Ami Jan, why are some mangoes going into pretty pots?"

Ami Jan was busy tossing spices into different pots. She tossed some fenugreek seeds into a pot before answering me. "Well, Lali, the big vats are for us to eat, and the prettier pots are to give to our guests."

"But why can't we keep the pretty ones? The ones with the good pieces."

Ami Jan's lips curled up into a smile as she turned to another pot with some pepper seeds. "Well, doesn't it make you feel good and special when you visit someone's house and the person gives you the very best? That's how we tell guests they are important to us. We give them our very best."

The younger kids played in the backyard, amongst the lemon trees while I watched the women making chutney. They were serious,

"Well, doesn't it make you feel good and special when you visit someone's house and the person gives you the very best? That's how we tell guests they are important to us. We give them our very best."

focused on their task, looking up only once in a while to tuck an errant tendril of hair behind their ears or swat a fly away. My job was to keep the children (and flies) away from the tantalizing mango pieces. Every so often, they would sneak up and try to steal a taste, just one little piece. But I would scold them and send them back to the yard. Sometimes if Ami Jan was sweating, I would bring her a washcloth and wipe her face.

Bi Ji glanced at Ami Jan often with approving looks as they mixed and poured and assembled the concoction into the clay pots. Bi Ji felt blessed that her son was married to such a talented, efficient, and learned woman. The thin cotton of their kamiz rippled once in a while if there was a breeze. It was hot, but since there were no men around, the women could go without dupattas. When the mango pickles were finished at the end of the day, they covered the pots with cheesecloth to sit for a few weeks. The woman would occasionally stir it, but mostly, it would just sit and be left on its own to finish pickling.

The chutney was prepared first on the stove and then stored in sterilized airtight jars. Samania was my favorite (see page 23). It was golden and sweet and sour, with peppers and raisins that would bubble to a lovely boil on the stove. It was beautiful to look at and to taste.

The pickles and chutneys were put away to be relished the entire year until the next season.

Badshahi Mosque, second largest mosque in the world, Lahore, Pakistan

Meat Dishes

Chicken Curry*

Lamb Curry*

Koftas (Meatballs) Curry

Bhuna Keema* (Not So Sloppy Joe)

Beef Curry*

Pakistani people love meat. We love chicken and wild birds, lamb and goat, and beef. The animals we eat must be qualified as consumable or halal. They have to be slaughtered in a way that is hygienic and does not cause the animal too much suffering. Animals must not be carnivores. Only herbivores are eaten. Herbivores lie lower on the food chain, subsisting on grass and plant life. As a biologist, I understand that the lower an animal is on the food chain, the less concentrated the toxins in its meat. By eating only the animals that graze in the fields or feed on the algae or plankton of the sea and by using halal methods of slaughtering and preparation, we maintain traditions that have existed to protect us for generations.

* Gluten free

CHICKEN CURRY*

Ingredients
2 medium onions, diced (about 2 cups)
¼ cup olive oil
1 small skinless chicken (2–3 pounds), cut into 8–12 pieces
7–10 cloves garlic, crushed into a paste
4 teaspoons ground red pepper (depending on taste)
2 teaspoons ground cumin
½ teaspoon ground turmeric
1–2 teaspoons salt (depending on taste)
1 teaspoon ginger, crushed or ground
4 teaspoons ground coriander
2 medium tomatoes, chopped (about 1 cup)
½ cup yogurt
½ cup fresh cilantro for garnish, finely chopped

Procedure
1. In a medium saucepan, sauté the onions in oil until light brown. Transfer onions to a separate dish, making sure to leave the oil in the pan.
2. Add chicken and garlic to remaining oil. Cook over medium heat until all of the liquid evaporates (chicken will release water as it cooks). Do not let it stick to the pan while cooking.
3. Add sautéed onions and ½ cup water to the chicken. Cook over medium heat for 10–20 minutes. Stir a few times during this step to make sure that it does not stick to the bottom of the pan.
4. Add salt, all of the spices, chopped tomatoes, and yogurt to chicken. Cook uncovered over medium heat for approximately 15–20 minutes. Again, let the water

evaporate. The spices, onions, and tomatoes will mix together and form a lumpy paste. We call this paste masala, and it is the basis of much of our cooking.

5. Add ¼ cup water. Stir, cover, and let simmer on low heat for approximately 10 minutes.

6. Transfer to serving dish and garnish with cilantro.

Tip: Serve with steamed rice, rice pilaf, or flatbread.

LAMB CURRY*

Ingredients

2 pounds lamb chops or lamb shank, cut into 2- to 3-inch pieces
4 medium onions, chopped (roughly 3 cups chopped)
10 cloves garlic
4 teaspoons crushed coriander seeds
4 teaspoons ground red pepper
2 teaspoons cumin seeds, crushed
½ teaspoon ground turmeric
1–2 teaspoons salt
4 medium tomatoes, chopped (roughly 2 cups)
2 tablespoon vegetable oil
½ cup fresh cilantro leaves, to garnish

Procedure

1. Remove all visible fat from the lamb pieces.
2. In a medium saucepan with a heavy bottom, add lamb, onions, garlic, and 2 cups of water. Place on medium heat and bring to a boil.
3. Lower heat, cover, and let simmer for 30–50 minutes until the meat is easily breakable with a knife. Larger pieces will take longer to become tender. Make sure it does not burn.
4. Remove the lid, stir, and add all of the spices, salt, tomatoes, and oil.
5. Keep on stirring and scraping the bottom on medium heat until the onions, garlic, and tomatoes become sauce-like (masala).

6. Add ½ cup water and bring to a boil. Turn the heat to low, cover, and let simmer for 10 minutes.

7. Garnish with cilantro leaves.

Tip: Serve over a bed of rice or with flatbread. Also, you may add peas, chopped potatoes, fried okra, squash, or bitter melon with ½ cup water and cook covered on medium to low heat for another 5–10 minutes. Vegetable cooking times vary.

KOFTAS (MEATBALLS) CURRY

Ingredients
For Koftas
1 pound ground turkey, beef, or lamb

2 medium onions, finely ground in a food processor,
    about 2 cups

2 teaspoons garlic powder or 6 cloves crushed

2 teaspoons ground red pepper (amount depends on desired
    hotness)

1–2 teaspoons garam masala (amount depends on desired
    hotness)

1 teaspoon salt

½ cup breadcrumbs

For Masala
¼ cup of oil

2 medium onions, finely chopped, about 2 cups

7 cloves garlic, crushed

3 teaspoons ground coriander

3 teaspoons ground red pepper

2 teaspoons cumin seeds

½ teaspoon ground turmeric

1–2 teaspoons salt

Peeled and chopped tomatoes, about 1 cup

1 2-inch-square piece of ginger, cut into very thin strips

For Garnish
½ cup cilantro, chopped

Procedure

1. **For koftas:** In a glass bowl, mix ground meat, onions, and the remaining ingredients. Divide the mixture into 15–20 portions. Use water to moisten your hands so the meat will not stick. Make golf-ball-sized meatballs or koftas. Set aside on a plate.

2. **For masala:** In a medium saucepan, heat the oil over medium heat. Add onions and garlic and sauté until light brown. Add ½ cup water, bring to a boil, and cover. Let simmer on low heat 10–15minutes.

3. Remove lid and either mash the onions using a metallic potato masher or grind using a food processor. Add coriander, red pepper, cumin seeds, turmeric, salt, and tomatoes to the onions.

4. Cook and stir for 5–10. When all of the water is evaporated and the oil seems to be separating from the sauce, your masala is ready.

5. **For curry:** Turn the heat to medium and lower one kofta at a time into the masala, making sure not to break them. Let cook on one side for a few minutes and then gently turn them to the other side. The koftas will become firm enough to be turned without breaking. Cook for 10–20 more minutes, stirring and scraping the bottom of the pan until the oil seems to be separating from the masala.

6. Add 1 cup water. Bring to a boil and let simmer for 10 minutes on low heat. Turn off the heat. Add ginger pieces. Cover and let sit for a few minutes before serving.

7. Transfer to a serving dish and garnish with cilantro.

Tip: Can be prepared in advance and stored in the refrigerator for a day or freezer for up to a week.

BHUNA KEEMA*
(NOT SO SLOPPY JOE)
I find this dish one of the easiest to make!

Ingredients

$1/8$ cup oil

2 pounds ground turkey, lamb, or beef

2 cups chopped onions

5 cloves garlic

3 teaspoons ground coriander

3 teaspoons ground red pepper

2 teaspoons ground cumin

½ teaspoon ground turmeric

1 teaspoon salt

2 medium tomatoes, finely cut, about 1 cup

2 teaspoons crushed ginger

½ cup finely chopped cilantro leaves to garnish

2 teaspoons tomato paste

Procedure

1. In a heavy-bottomed, small saucepan, add the oil and the ground meat. Cook over medium heat for 10 minutes. Use a spatula to break any meat clumps that may form. Set aside.

2. Using a food processor or blender, grind the onion and the garlic with 2 tablespoons of water.

3. Add the ground spices, salt, and ground onions and garlic to the meat.

4. Stir and cook uncovered over high to medium heat, scraping the bottom occasionally for 20–30 minutes until the meat changes color and almost all of the water is evaporated.

5. Add tomato paste and crushed ginger and cook another 10–20 minutes.
6. Turn the heat off. Cover and let sit for a few minutes
7. Garnish with cilantro.

Tip: You may add peas, chopped potatoes, beans, bell peppers, or bitter melon with ½ cup water and cook covered on medium to low heat for another 5–10 minutes.

BEEF CURRY*

Ingredients

2 pounds beef, any cut, preferably with bone as it makes a richer
    gravy, cut into 2- to 4-inch pieces
2 medium onions, chopped, about 2 cups
10 cloves garlic
4 teaspoons crushed coriander seeds
2 teaspoons ground red pepper
2 teaspoon crushed cumin seeds
½ teaspoon ground turmeric
1–2 teaspoons salt
2 medium tomatoes, chopped, about 1 cup
2-inch piece of ginger root, peeled and thinly sliced
¼ cup vegetable oil
½ cup fresh cilantro, to garnish

Procedure

1. In a medium-sized, heavy-bottomed saucepan, add beef, onions, garlic, and 1 cup water. Place on medium heat and bring to a boil.

2. Lower heat, cover, and let simmer for 20–30 minutes, making sure it does not burn. Add more water if needed.

3. Remove the lid, stir, and add all spices, salt, tomatoes, ginger, and oil.

4. Keep on stirring and scraping the bottom on medium heat until the onions, garlic, and tomatoes form a sauce (called masala).

5. Add ½ cup water. Bring to a boil .Turn the heat to low, cover, and let simmer for 10 minutes.

6. Garnish with cilantro.

Tip: Serve over a bed of rice or with flatbread.

KITTO AND I AND THE
WEDDING FEAST
Summer 1965

I was sitting in my eleventh grade physics final. Kitto, my best friend and partner in crime for many years, was in the same class. We had studied all year for this test, which did not finish until four o'clock.

For several weeks, we had been anxiously looking forward to the test being over, not only because we would be done with physics studies for the year but also because we looked forward to the wedding feast of my cousin, Javeed Bahi. Pakistani wedding feasts are legendary. Pakistani people love an opportunity to share food in celebration. The previous night, while I crammed for my test, special chefs went to my cousin's to prepare huge dishes of chicken korma, spinach with goat meat, yogurt ryta, fresh sesame naan, and zurda for dessert.

My mind was thinking about the test, but my stomach was thinking about the wedding feast.

My father's sister (we called her Phophoo) loved me and had told me a few days before the luncheon, "By the time you come home, food will be waiting for you in your kitchen." She did not want to me to go all the way to her house and waste precious studying time. She sent one of the servants on the bus with lots of food for Kitto and me.

After the exam, we rushed home (this took us an hour or so since the college was far away). We found the house empty and the kitchen padlocked. We could smell the savory aromas of the food my aunt had promised. I knew where the key would be so Kitto and I rushed to the hiding spot. We were starving, and the aromas of the wedding feast wafted through the verandah. But there was no key anywhere.

Pakistani wedding feasts are legendary. Pakistani people love an opportunity to share food in celebration.

No phone to call Ami Jan or Phophoo. No one to offer any solution or information. Kitto found a brick in one of the coal pits in the courtyard and had the idea to break the lock. We tried, but the brick broke in two pieces. I ran to my brother's room to find his toolbox for a hammer. That worked. We got into the kitchen and enjoyed the feast, filling ourselves up with scrumptious chicken and breads and rice dishes until we could not eat any more and dozed off on the verandah. Soon Kitto's niece came to remind her to come home to her family, and my family started coming home.

Lala in wedding attire, Lahore, Pakistan, 1972

Fish

Soooo Quick Fish Curry*

Soooo Quick Shrimp Curry*

Fish Pakoras*

Fish Kabobs*

Fish is not a very common food away from coastal areas as it is quite expensive. Still, there are many fish shops and vendors that sell fish marinated in gram flour with special spices and then fried in mustard oil. Almost anyone can afford tandoori bread, a piece of fried fish with spicy daikon radish salad once in a while.

The city of Karachi is by the Indian Ocean. Saltwater fish is primarily consumed by the natives and the people in adjacent areas. In Lahore, which is a part of Punjab Province (punj means five, and ab means water), five rivers flow through it so there are many different kinds of freshwater fish caught and sold by the local fishermen. Since freezing and packaging facilities are not readily available, most of the fish is sold and consumed fresh.

* Gluten free

SOOOO QUICK FISH CURRY*

Ingredients

¾ cup yellow onion, chopped

4 tablespoons oil

1 cup plain yogurt

3 teaspoons ground coriander

3 teaspoons ground red pepper

1 teaspoon ground cumin

½ teaspoon ground turmeric

1 teaspoon salt

1–1½ pounds skinned white fish fillet, like cod or tilapia

½ cup chopped fresh cilantro for garnish

Procedure

1. Grind the onions with 2 tablespoons of water to a very fine paste in a food processor. Set aside.

2. In a heavy-bottomed pan, heat the oil over high to medium heat.

3. Add the onions. Stir and scrape the bottom and cook until the onion paste turns yellow. This will not take more than 10–15 minutes.

4. Add all of the rest of the ingredients except the fish and cilantro. Cook until all of the water is evaporated (the yogurt will release water). Stir and scrape the pan's bottom continuously during this step. Continue until you end up with a good masala, where the oil seems to be leaving the sauce.

5. Just before serving the meal, gently lower the fish filet on top of the masala. Cook on both sides, about 3–5 minutes each side.

6. Turn off the heat. Cover and let sit.

7. Using a spatula, transfer the fish and the masala to a serving dish and garnish with cilantro.

Tip: Goes well with steamed basmati rice.

SOOOO QUICK SHRIMP CURRY*

Ingredients

½ cup yellow onion, chopped

¼ cup oil

2 teaspoon mango powder

2 teaspoons ground coriander

2 teaspoons ground red pepper

1 teaspoon roasted cumin seeds

1 teaspoon salt

½ cup plain yoghurt

1–1½ pounds deveined and peeled shrimp

½ cup cilantro, finely chopped, to garnish

Procedure

1. In a heavy-bottomed pan, heat the oil over high to medium heat.

2. Add the onions. Stir and cook until the onion turns translucent. This will not take more than 5 minutes.

3. Add all of the rest of the ingredients except the shrimp and cilantro. Cook on low heat for a few minutes. Do not let it burn.

4. Set the prepared masala aside until just before you are ready to serve the mean. Then add the shrimp to the masala and cook on high heat for 3–5 minutes.

5. Turn off the heat. Do not cover.

6. Using a spatula, transfer the shrimp and the masala to a serving dish and garnish with cilantro.

Tip: Goes well with steamed basmati rice or as an appetizer.

FISH PAKORAS*

Ingredients

1 pound tilapia or any other white fish, cut into1- to 2-inch thick
pieces

2–4 tablespoons lemon juice

1 cup gram flour (also known as besan, available at Asian or
Middle Eastern food stores)

½ teaspoon baking soda

1 teaspoon salt

2 teaspoons cayenne pepper

4 teaspoons ground coriander

1 teaspoon roasted cumin seeds

½ cup water

1 cup oil

Procedure

1. Wet both sides of the fish pieces with lemon juice. Set aside.

2. In a bowl, mix gram flour, baking soda, salt, cayenne,
    coriander, cumin seeds, and water. Mixture should have the
    consistency of pancake batter. Set aside.

3. In a large skillet, heat oil over medium heat. Oil should
    cover the bottom of the pan completely and be
    approximately 1 inch in depth. Test if oil is hot enough by
    dropping ½ teaspoon of batter into it; if batter sizzles, oil is
    at appropriate temperature.

4. Pat dry the fish pieces and dip two to three pieces of fish
    into the gram-flour mixture. Be sure to coat both sides of
    each piece well. Gently place into hot oil and fry both sides
    until coating appears golden brown. Remove from oil and
    place on paper towels to absorb excess oil. Repeat till all
    fish pieces are done.

Tip: Tastes great with salsa or mint chutney.

FISH KABOBS*

Ingredients

1 14-ounce can salmon

4 teaspoons ground coriander

3 teaspoons ground red pepper

2 teaspoons ground cumin

½–1 teaspoon salt

½ cup onions or scallions, finely chopped

½ cup cilantro leaves, finely chopped

½ cup breadcrumbs or Asian rice flakes

½ cup vegetable oil

1 egg, well beaten

Procedure

1. Drain and rinse the canned salmon.
2. Mix all spices, salt, onions, cilantro, and breadcrumbs with the fish.
3. Divide the fish mixture into 10–15 golf-ball-sized balls.
4. Flatten each ball into ½- to1-inch-thick cake. Set aside.
5. In a heavy-bottomed pan, heat the oil over low to medium heat.
6. Dip 4–6 cakes at one time in beaten egg. Gently lower into the hot oil.
7. Cook both sides until golden brown.
8. Remove kabobs from oil. Let drain on paper towels.
9. Serve warm with mint or tamarind chutney.

Tip: This is an excellent filling for any kind of sandwiches. Great as an appetizer!

AROOJ THE MUCHALI WALLA

My youngest daughter, Arooj, was always a mischievous little thing. When she and Ann were small, I used to try to get them to take a nap during the day. We would climb up into the bed together and snuggle up. Ann would fall fast asleep in no time. Arooj, though, would often pretend to fall asleep and sneak off as soon as she thought we were sleeping.

One afternoon, in our tiny Pakistan apartment, Ann and I had just fallen to sleep when I was woken by strange sounds coming from the kitchen. I lifted my head and put my hand on the bed next to me and discovered Arooj was missing. I gently got up from the bed so as not to awaken Ann and padded into the kitchen to see what Roojie was up to.

Now, Arooj was a renowned copycat. One day, I came into the bathroom to find her trying to pull out her teeth. "What are you doing?" I asked. She pulled her fingers out of her mouth and said, "Putting my teeth in a cup like Ami Jan does."

Crashes and bangs were coming from the kitchen in what was, no doubt, the makeshift cymbals of a child gotten into Mommy's pots and pans. I poked my head around the kitchen door. There was Arooj, cross-legged on the cement floor, all of my pots and pans, dragged from their places on the bottom shelf, circled around her.

"What are you doing, Rooji?"

"I'm a muchali walla, Mommy!" she announced proudly.

"You are? Well, right now, it is time for muchali walla to take a nap so they can sell more fish." I tried to scold, but a smile was creeping into my voice.

"But, Mommy, . . ."

"Come, Arooj. After our nap, I will teach you how to make fish like the muchali walla."

My muchali walla still loves to cook and entertain friends and family whenever she has some spare time from her busy schedule. Not having a dining table is no problem. She can lay out a beautiful table right on the carpet in her living room.

Lala's daughter Arooj preparing food for friends, Seattle, Washington, 2010

Friends of Lala's daughter Arooj and the Pakistani feast she and Lala prepared, Seattle, Washington, 2009

Rytas and Salads

Potatoes Ryta*

Cucumber Ryta*

Kuchumar Salad*

Gluten free

POTATOES RYTA*

Ingredients

4 small potatoes

1 cup plain yogurt

1 tablespoon finely chopped onion

1 tablespoon finely chopped cilantro or mint leaves

½ teaspoon salt

1 teaspoon crushed black or red pepper

1 small tomato, finely chopped, for garnish

Procedure

1. Peel and cut each potato into 4 pieces. Cook the potato pieces in boiling water until fork tender.

2. Remove from heat, drain, and set aside to cool.

3. In a serving bowl, mix the rest of the ingredients, except for the tomatoes, with the cooled potatoes. Mix well and garnish with chopped tomatoes.

Tip: Eat it with spicy curries to reduce the heat.

CUCUMBER RYTA*

Ingredients
2 small cucumbers, sliced
2 teaspoons salt
1 cup yogurt
1 medium tomato, chopped
2 scallions, sliced
1 teaspoon cayenne (optional)
Cilantro or parsley leaves, chopped, for garnish

Procedure
1. Sprinkle cucumber slices with salt and let sit for 5 minutes. Rinse under running water, squeezing the slices gently.
2. Combine remaining ingredients, except cilantro or parsley, with cucumbers and stir. Garnish with chopped cilantro or parsley leaves.

Tip: Great for hot summer days with rice pilau or curries.

KUCHUMAR SALAD*

Kuchumar means "beaten to a pulp." In this salad, every item is chopped into ½- or ¼-inch pieces, or even smaller.

Ingredients
6–8 large salad leaves (preferably romaine)
1 medium onion
4 plum or medium tomatoes
6 small red radishes
2 small cucumbers
½ cup chopped cilantro
¼ cup chopped mint leaves
1 teaspoon salt
1 teaspoon ground red pepper
Juice of 1 lemon

Procedure
1. Wash and pat dry salad leaves. Chop into 1- to 2-inch-size pieces.
2. Peel and chop the onion into small, raisin-size pieces.
3. Wash and chop tomatoes and radishes into raisin-size pieces.
4. Wash and, if desired, peel the cucumbers and chop into raisin-size pieces.
5. In a mixing bowl, combine all salad ingredients from steps 1–4, plus the cilantro and mint leaves.
6. Mix salt and pepper in lemon juice and mix with the salad.

Tip: This salad goes well with all kinds of food.

ANN AND THE LELLO BUTTER

Shortly after my first daughter, Ann, was born, we moved to England so my husband could study for his PhD in endocrinology.

About three years later, we moved back to Pakistan. One Sunday, we were at my mother's, enjoying one of those breakfasts that never ends but just keeps going into the afternoon. My mom had prepared minced meat and eggs and parathas, but there was also sliced bread.

Ann, my proper little British lady, refused to butter her toast with the butter Ami Jan brought her. In England, butter is made from cow's cream and is yellow, but in Pakistan, because it is made from buffalo cream, butter is white. The whole family was there, enjoying Ann's dramatic and emphatic refusal.

Ann stuck her chin out, "I want lello butter!"

Ami Jan said to Ann, "Oh, you want yellow butter? I have yellow butter in the kitchen." She scooted back to the kitchen, her silky shalwar, kamiz, and dupatta rippling in her wake. She slipped some turmeric from the pantry and expertly whipped it into the butter to make it "lello."

When Ami Jan came back to the table, Ann happily buttered her toast with lello butter.

You cannot explain cultural differences to a four-year-old.

Lala and daughter Ann, Birmingham, England, 1977

Egg Dishes

Plain Egg Omelet*

Boiled Eggs with Keema*

Scrambled Eggs, Potatoes,
and Peas or Bell Pepper*

Gluten free

PLAIN EGG OMELET*

Ingredients
4–6 eggs
2 tablespoons milk
½ cup finely chopped onion
¼ cup finely chopped cilantro
1 teaspoon ground red pepper
Salt to taste
2 tablespoons oil

Procedure
1. Beat the eggs and milk using a fork until well beaten.
2. Add the rest of the ingredients except oil.
3. In a nonstick or stainless steel frying pan, heat the oil over medium heat.
4. Pour the egg mixture and, using a spatula, spread it over the whole pan.
5. When eggs start firming up around the edges, fold the sides and try to make it fish shaped. Cook both sides until golden brown.

Tip: Tastes great with a paratha.

BOILED EGGS WITH KEEMA*

Ingredients
6 hard-boiled eggs
All ingredients needed for Bhuna Keema

Procedure
1. Prepare your keema according to the recipe in Bhuna Keema (page 36).
2. Transfer the Bhuna Keema to a serving dish.
3. Cut each egg lengthwise and place all twelve pieces (yolk side up) around the periphery of the dish.

Tip: This dish is excellent for brunches. The yellow yolk against the dark minced meat is also visually stunning.

SCRAMBLED EGGS, POTATOES, AND PEAS OR BELL PEPPER*

Ingredients

4–6 small red potatoes (1 pound)
¼ cup oil
1 cup onion, finely chopped
4 eggs, well beaten
4 teaspoons ground coriander
2 teaspoons ground red pepper
1 teaspoon ground cumin
½ cup frozen peas OR ½ cup seeded and finely diced bell
   pepper
Cilantro or mint, chopped, for garnish; optional

Procedure

1. Peel and dice potatoes into ½- to 1-inch-size pieces.
2. In a heavy-bottomed skillet, over low to medium heat, heat the oil and cook potatoes for 7–10 minutes until almost soft. Stir frequently.
3. Add chopped onions and bell peppers, if using. Cook for 2–3 minutes until the onions are translucent.
4. Add eggs and the rest of the ingredients, including peas if using instead of bell pepper, but not garnish. Cook a few more minutes, stirring frequently.
5. Cook a few more minutes until the eggs are soft scrambled.
6. Transfer to a serving dish and garnish with cilantro or mint, if desired.

Tip: Ideal dish for brunches or a quick dinner. At this point, my daughter Ann insists I add her definite preference for peas.

THE EGG VENDOR'S WIT

When I was growing up, my father insisted we enjoy dinner together as a family. My brothers and sister would gather around the table and tell stories from our day. The ones told by my eldest brother, Nadir, were often particularly entertaining. One night, he regaled us with a tale about his meeting with the egg vendor. Nadir had come upon the vendor on his walk home from high school and thought he would purchase a dozen eggs as a special treat. At six feet one inch, Nadir was already taller than most boys his age and even grown men.

Nadir told us how he had tried to bargain a better price with the egg vendor. I could imagine his long shadow hovering over the vendor's low wooden table.

"Well," Ami Jan, my mother, asked, "did you bring me any eggs?"

Nadir sat back in his chair. "I told him he was charging too much for such small eggs."

"And? Did you get them for cheaper?" Abi Jan, my father, asked.

A wide grin cracked across Nadir's face. "No, he just took a long puff off his hookah and said, 'No wonder they look small; you're looking at them from such a great height!'"

Vegetables

Eggplant and Potato Curry*

Cauliflower and Potato Curry*

Squash or Zucchini Curry*

Lala's Special Spinach Saag

Okra (Lady Fingers) Curry*

Mixed Vegetable Curry*

To prepare these vegetable curries, I have simplified the procedures by using almost the same ingredients for masala and following similar steps. Once you have mastered the preparation of masala, you can make your own variations.

* Gluten free

EGGPLANT AND POTATO CURRY*

Ingredients

¼ cup vegetable or olive oil

1 medium onion, chopped

1 teaspoon salt

4 cloves garlic, crushed

3 teaspoons ground coriander

3 teaspoons ground red pepper

1 teaspoon ground cumin seeds

½ teaspoon ground turmeric

2 medium tomatoes, seeded, peeled, and chopped

½ pound (or 4 small) red potatoes, peeled (or leave the skin on) and chopped into 2- to 3-inch pieces

1 small eggplant (roughly 1 pound), peeled and chopped into 2- to 3-inch pieces

½ cup fresh cilantro leaves, chopped, for garnish

Procedure

1. In a heavy-bottomed skillet, heat oil over medium heat.

2. Fry onion until translucent/golden brown. Add ½ cup water, bring to a boil, cover, and let simmer for 5 minutes. If the heat is too high, turn it down. Use a potato masher to crush the onions.

3. To prepare masala, add salt, garlic, coriander, red pepper, cumin, turmeric, and tomatoes to the crushed onion.

4. Cook for 5–10 minutes, stirring and scraping the bottom of the pan constantly. Continue until the water from the tomatoes has evaporated and oil starts to separate from masala.

5. Add potatoes and eggplant and ¼ cup water. Stir thoroughly.

6. Cover and cook over low heat until potatoes are soft. Scrape the bottom of the pan a few times during this step to prevent the masala from sticking to the bottom.

7. Transfer to a serving dish, and garnish with cilantro leaves

Tips: Serve with steamed basmati rice, chapatti, or other flatbread. This can be prepared in advance and stored in a refrigerator for up to 3–4 days.

CAULIFLOWER AND POTATO CURRY*

Ingredients
¼ cup vegetable or olive oil
1 medium onion, chopped
1 teaspoon salt
4 cloves garlic, crushed
3 teaspoons ground coriander
3 teaspoons ground red pepper
1 teaspoon ground cumin seeds
½ teaspoon ground turmeric
½ pound (or 4 small) red potatoes, peeled and chopped into
    2- to 3-inch pieces
3 cups cauliflower (roughly 1 pound), cut into small, 2- to 3-inch
    florets
½ cup fresh cilantro leaves, chopped, for garnish
1-inch piece of ginger, finely chopped, for garnish

Procedure
1. In a heavy-bottom skillet, heat oil over medium to high heat.
2. Fry onion until golden brown. Add ½ cup water, bring to a
    boil, cover, and let simmer for 10 minutes. If the heat is too
    high, turn it down. Use a potato masher to crush the onions.
3. To prepare masala, add salt, garlic, coriander, red pepper,
    cumin, and turmeric to the crushed onion.
4. Cook for 5 minutes, stirring and scraping the bottom of the
    pan constantly. Continue until oil starts to separate from
    masala.
5. Add potatoes and cauliflower and ¼ cup water. Stir
    thoroughly.
6. Cover and cook over low heat until potatoes are soft. Scrape

the bottom of the pan a few times during this step to prevent the masala from sticking to the bottom. If there seems to be standing water at this point, turn the heat to high and, while stirring so the curry will not stick to the pan, cook for a few minutes.

7. Transfer to a serving dish and garnish with cilantro and ginger.

Tip: Serve with flatbread. Traditionally, we do not eat rice with cauliflower.

SQUASH OR ZUCCHINI CURRY*

Ingredients

1/4 cup vegetable or olive oil

1 medium onion, chopped

4 cloves garlic, crushed

3 teaspoons ground coriander

3 teaspoons ground red pepper

1 teaspoon ground cumin seeds

½ teaspoon ground turmeric

1 teaspoon salt

1 pound or 4–6 small squash or zucchini, peeled and chopped into thin pieces. If using tender, organic squash or zucchini, you may prepare without peeling them to retain more nutrients.

½ cup fresh cilantro leaves, chopped for garnish

Procedure

1. In a heavy-bottom skillet, heat oil over medium to heat.
2. Fry chopped onion until golden brown. Add ½ cup water, bring to a boil, cover, and let simmer for 5 minutes. You may

have to play with the heat, depending on your stovetop. Use a potato masher to crush the onions.

3. To prepare masala, add garlic, coriander, red pepper, cumin, turmeric, and salt to the crushed onion.

4. Cook for 5–10 minutes, stirring and scraping the bottom of the pan constantly. Continue until oil starts to separate from masala.

5. Add squash or zucchini. Stir thoroughly.

6. Cover and cook over very low heat until squash pieces are soft (but not mashed). Scrape the bottom of the pan a few times during this step to prevent the masala from sticking to the bottom.

7. Transfer to a serving dish and garnish with cilantro.

Tip: Serve with steamed basmati rice, chapatti, or other flatbread.

LALI'S SPECIAL SPINACH SAAG

Ingredients

¼ cup vegetable oil

1 small onion, minced

7 cloves garlic, chopped

4 teaspoons ground coriander

3 teaspoons ground red pepper

1 teaspoon ground cumin seeds

½ teaspoon ground turmeric

1 teaspoon salt

2 pounds fresh spinach leaves, washed and finely chopped, or one 8-ounce package cut, frozen spinach

½ pound broccoli pieces, washed and cut into small pieces/florets, or ½ of an 8-ounce package frozen broccoli

2 teaspoons yellow or white corn flour or cornmeal (for thickening)

¼ cup vegetable oil

3 cloves garlic, minced

1- to 2-inch piece of ginger, finely chopped

Procedure

1. In a heavy-bottom skillet, heat oil over medium to low heat.

2. Fry onion until translucent/golden brown. Add ½ cup water, bring to a boil, cover, and let simmer for 10 minutes. If the heat is too high, please adjust it. Use a potato masher to crush the onion.

3. To prepare masala, add the 7 garlic cloves, coriander, red pepper, cumin, turmeric, and salt to the crushed onion.

4. Cook for 5–10 minutes, stirring and scraping the bottom of the pan constantly. Continue until oil starts to separate from masala.

5. Add spinach and broccoli. Mix thoroughly. Spinach and broccoli will release water, so no need to add water. Cover and cook over medium heat for about 15 minutes. Stir a few times so it does not stick to the bottom.

6. Remove cover, cook over medium heat, stirring frequently until almost all of the liquid has evaporated.

7. Add corn flour and mix thoroughly, making sure no lumps are formed. Saag should have a creamy consistency. Add ginger and mix it well.

8. Remove from heat. Cover and let sit.

9. Meanwhile, in a small frying pan, heat second ¼ cup oil over low heat. Add minced garlic and cook until garlic is golden brown, approximately 1–2 minutes. Remove from heat.

10. Transfer the saag to a serving dish. Drizzle the hot oil and garlic over the saag.

Tip: Serve with rice or flatbread. To make it even more delicious and richer, you may use chicken broth, instead of water, to cook.

OKRA (LADY FINGERS) CURRY*

Ingredients
½ cup vegetable oil, divided
1 cup yellow onion, diced
1 teaspoon salt
7 cloves garlic, crushed, or 2 teaspoons garlic powder
4 teaspoons ground coriander
3 teaspoons ground red pepper
2 teaspoons ground cumin
½ teaspoon ground turmeric
4 red tomatoes, peeled, seeded, and chopped
2 pounds fresh okra, washed and patted dry, ends removed and
    discarded, and cut into 1- to 2-inch pieces
Garam masala or black pepper for garnish

Procedure
1. In a heavy-bottomed skillet, heat ¼ cup oil over medium to low heat.
2. Fry half of the chopped onions until golden brown. Add ½ cup water, bring to a boil, cover, and let simmer for 5 minutes. Adjust heat as needed. Use a potato masher to crush the onions.
3. To prepare masala, add salt, garlic, coriander, red pepper, cumin, turmeric, and tomatoes to the crushed onion.
4. Cook for 5–10 minutes, stirring and scraping the bottom of the pan constantly. Continue until oil starts to separate from masala. Set aside.
5. In a separate skillet, heat the other ¼ cup oil over medium heat and add prepped okra.

6. Sauté the okra on high to medium heat, stirring frequently so it is evenly cooked, until all of the sticky juices from the okra become dry. Remove the okra from the skillet and set aside. This process will take at least 15–20 minutes

7. Add rest of the onion and sautéed okra to the masala. Stir, cover, and let simmer over low heat for 5–10 minutes

8. Transfer to a serving dish and garnish with garam masala or black pepper

Tip: Do not use frozen okra or it will be slimy. Okra must be fresh, green (no brown spots), and tender, the smaller the better!

MIXED VEGETABLE CURRY*

Ingredients

1/4 cup plus 2 tablespoons oil
1 cup chopped onion
1–2 teaspoons salt
4 cloves garlic, peeled and crushed
3 teaspoons ground red pepper
3 teaspoons ground coriander
2 teaspoons ground cumin
½ teaspoon ground turmeric
1 cup chopped tomatoes
2 cups cauliflower, cut into 1- to 2-inch pieces/florets
1 cup frozen peas
2 cups carrots, peeled and diced into ¼- to ½-inch pieces
2 cups potatoes, cut into 1- to 2-inch pieces
Fresh cilantro or mint for garnish

Procedure

1. In a heavy-bottom skillet, heat ¼ cup oil over medium to low heat.
2. Fry onion until golden brown. Add ½ cup water, bring to a boil, cover, and let simmer for 10 minutes. Use a potato masher to crush the onions.
3. To prepare masala, add salt, garlic, red pepper, coriander, cumin, turmeric, and tomatoes to the crushed onions.
4. Cook for 5–10 minutes, stirring and scraping the bottom of the pan constantly. Continue until oil starts to separate from masala. Set aside.
5. In a separate skillet, heat 2 tablespoons oil. Sauté the rest of the ingredients except garnish for 5–10 minutes.
6. Add to the prepared masala. Also add ¼ cup water.

7. Bring the mixture to a boil and let simmer, covered, for 10 minutes. Scrape the bottom a few times so the masala does not stick to the bottom. Turn off the heat and let sit 5–10 minutes. Remove to the serving dish and garnish with cilantro or mint.

Tip: You may use frozen vegetables, but not canned.

A FAMILY GARDEN

Vegetable vendors were frequent characters during my youth in Pakistan. From as far back as I can remember, I would see them hauling the bounty they had collected from nearby farms. They carried their cornucopias on horse carts, on the backs of bicycles, or even sometimes, in huge straw baskets perched on their heads.

The women of past generations, and even still today, would open their doors daily to the vendors. Whatever came out of the vendor's basket was what they cooked that day for their family.

Food vendor in Lahore, Pakistan, 2005

I used to love the surprise of what might show up on our dinner table. What treasure had Ami Jan won from a vendor and cleverly folded into a curry? During the winter months, we had various versions of turnip, cauliflower, spinach, or green peas with potatoes. All curries were served with fresh flatbread or rice, different kinds of dals, and a chutney or pickle.

There being no supermarket to run to, the other options for food were what we grew ourselves or purchased from various small food shops. My family had a plot of garden at my grandfather's house. Aba Ji's house sat in the middle of a large patch of land. My dear mango trees stood on one side of the house, and on the other was a field that Aba Ji split into four sections. Aba Ji designated an area to grow vegetables for our family. I loved the location of our vegetable garden since it was closer to the small sugar cane plot and under the shade of a tall date tree.

We grew many things, depending on the season—turnips, squash, radishes, cauliflower, and too many herbs to count. Water was scarce so we ran pipes or channels to redirect the water from the shower and the kitchen (water from the dishwasher). We split our drinking and showering water with the plants in the fields. Sometimes I helped Ami Jan spread or push seeds into the earth and cover them with little dirt mounds. It was a joy to watch for the tiny sprouts to begin poking their little green arms up from the earth. I could not help but giggle when I heard my aunt's exasperated screams when my ever-hungry brothers had gotten into her turnips, peas, or carrots.

We had a gardener who came every day, early morning or early evening to avoid the sun's more brutal hours. He was a tall man, older, but handsome, with a healthy glow from the sun. He was amazing. One day I watched as he cut a whole acre field with a scythe in half an hour.

He also tended the vines and bushes that covered the house. I especially remember the glorious bougainvillea with its great fuchsia-colored blooms. He also worked the great grape vine that wrapped around almost the entire house. In summer, it was heavy and falling with grapes. We would cover them with cloth sacks to keep the birds from eating them. We color-coded the sacks by family. My family's sacks were printed. My aunts' were solid colors. There was no refrigeration, no checking the fridge to see what was there to eat. Instead, we checked the trees, the ground, the fields, or the vines.

Every other morning of grape season, we would wake to my aunt's angry shouts as she discovered an empty sack that my naughty, younger brothers had ransacked. They managed to get to them despite my parents' scolding and warnings. They were growing, hungry boys after all.

Dals: Dried, Split Lentils and Beans

Dals Simplified

Common Recipe for All Types of Dal

Masoor Dal (Pink Lentils)*

Moong Dal (Yellow Lentils)*

Channa Dal (Yellow Dried Split Peas)*

Maash (Creamy Lentils) *

Vegetarian Haleem

Chickpea Curry*

Dals are the poor man's food but rich in nutrition for everyone.

One can easily substitute one dal for another in a recipe. You can buy lentils in bulk and store them in airtight containers in the pantry or refrigerator. They should last many months. Always add 1–2 teaspoons of oil when you start to cook lentils.

Gluten free

DALS SIMPLIFIED

There are many, many kinds of dals. This is a recipe that I use to cook almost all kinds. In this book, it applies to masoor, moong, chana, and maash dal, all in this section.

Garnishes are added after cooking to make the dal even tastier.

Dals are very sticky, especially maash dal, and easily stick to the bottom of the pan. They are so sticky that, in Ijaz's great-grandmother's house, they used it as mortar for bricks. Do not worry, though; follow my recipe and your pots and pans should be fine.

Cooking time may vary depending on the grain size and origin of the crop, etc.

Chickpeas are not dal, but I have included them in the chart because you soak and cook them(to soften) the same amount of time as the dals.

LALA'S DAL HARDNESS SCALE		
SOFT	**Soaking Time**	**Cooking Time**
1 cup Masoor	10 min.	30 min. in 2 cups of water
1 cup Moong	20 min.	40 min. in 3 cups of water
1 cup Channa	30 min.	50 min. in 4 cups of water
1 cup Maash	30 min.	50 min. in 4 cups of water
1 cup Masoor with husks	1 hr.	1 hr. in 5 cups of water
1 cup Moong with husks	1 hr.	1 hr. in 5 cups of water
1 cup Chickpeas	1 hr.	1 hr. in 5 cups of water
HARD		

From the top, clockwise:
— Red Dal or Masoor
— Yellow Dal or Moong
— White Dal or Maash
— Yellow Peas or Channa

COMMON RECIPE FOR ALL TYPES OF DAL

Masoor Dal (Pink Lentils)*
Moong Dal (Yellow Lentils)*
Channa Dal (Yellow Dried Split Peas)*
Maash (Creamy Lentils) *

Ingredients
1 cup dal
2 teaspoons ground red pepper
½ teaspoon ground turmeric
1 teaspoon salt
1 tablespoon vegetable or olive oil
Water (see chart on page 85, Dals Simplified, for how much
water for the lentils you have chosen)

Procedure
1. Place the dal in a sieve or colander and wash several times under running water. Washing dal is important as this removes impurities, like soil and little pieces of stones. Transfer dal to a pan and let soak for the requisite amount of time (see chart on page 85). Discard the water after soaking is done.

2. Place dal required amount of water (see chart) and the rest of the ingredients in a heavy-bottomed saucepan and stir thoroughly. Most dals boil over easily so make sure your saucepan is deep.

3. Bring the mixture to a boil over medium heat. Stir thoroughly.

4. Turn the heat to low and cook, partially covered, for the required amount of time (see chart on page 85). End result should be a little thick and soupy (like a runny split-pea soup). You might have to add more water if the dal gets too

thick or cook for few minutes on high heat if there is too much standing water. Do not let it stick to the bottom of the pan. Use a potato masher to mash roughly half of the dal in the pan at the end of this step.

5. Your dal is ready! Transfer to a serving dish. Finish with any number of the following herbs or spices prepared in the way described.

   a. Fry 1 teaspoon whole cumin seeds for 20 to 30 seconds in 2 tablespoons olive oil. Drizzle dal with fried cumin seeds and the oil in which it was fried. Make sure to add the oil as this imparts richness and depth of flavor.

   b. Fry 1 tablespoon finely chopped garlic in 2 tablespoons olive oil. Garlic should be light brown in color after frying. Drizzle dal with garlic and the oil in which it was fried. Make sure to add the oil as this imparts richness and depth of flavor.

   c. Fry ½ cup finely sliced onion in 3 tablespoons olive oil. Onions should be golden brown. Drizzle dal with onions and the oil in which they were fried to impart richness and depth of flavor.

   d. Add ½ cup finely chopped fresh cilantro leaves.

   e. For really brave cooks: add 1 tablespoon finely chopped hot green pepper of your choice.

   f. Use raw or fry peeled and grated 2-inch piece of ginger in 2 tablespoons of olive oil. Drizzle dal with ginger and the oil in which it was fried. Make sure to add the oil as this imparts richness and depth of flavor.

VEGETARIAN HALEEM

Ingredients
2 tablespoons husk-free moong dal
2 tablespoons husk-free chana dal
2 tablespoons husk-free masoor dal
2 tablespoons husk-free maash dal
2 tablespoons brown rice
2 tablespoons moong dal with husk
2 tablespoons masoor dal with husk
¼ cup vegetable oil, divided
2 teaspoons salt
3 teaspoons ground red pepper
2 tablespoons old-fashioned oatmeal
1 teaspoon whole cumin seeds
2-inch piece of ginger, very finely chopped
7 cloves garlic, finely chopped
Fresh cilantro, chopped

I use a slow cooker to prepare haleem. Dals can be sticky, and cooking them on the stovetop requires a great deal of attention. By using a slow cooker, I eliminate the need for this rather tedious preparation.

Procedure
1. Place the dals and brown rice in a sieve or colander and wash several times under running water. Washing dal is important as this removes impurities, like soil and little pieces of rock. Soak brown rice and dals for 2 hours.
2. To a slow cooker, add five cups of water, 2 tablespoons vegetable oil, salt, red pepper, and the dals and brown rice from step 1.

3. Let cook on high for 5 hours or on low for 8 hours.

4. Remove lid from slow cooker carefully, avoiding the steam. Add oatmeal and another cup of water. Stir thoroughly. Place the lid back.

5. Let cook for 1 hour on high. Turn the heat off. Stir thoroughly. The mixture will look mushy.

6. In a frying pan, use the remaining 2 tablespoons of oil to fry cumin seeds, ginger, and garlic for 1–2 minutes. Use low to medium heat. Fry till garlic and ginger are a beautiful light golden brown.

7. Pour contents of frying pan into the haleem and mix once or twice.

8. Place haleem in a serving dish and garnish with cilantro.

Tip: Haleem can stay fresh in a refrigerator for up to 1 week or in a freezer for 2–3 weeks.

CHICKPEA CURRY*

Ingredients

¼ cup vegetable oil,
1 cup yellow onion, chopped
1 teaspoon salt
7 cloves garlic, crushed, or 2 teaspoons garlic powder
3 teaspoons ground coriander
3 teaspoons ground red pepper
2 teaspoons ground cumin
½ teaspoon ground turmeric
4 red tomatoes, peeled and chopped, about 2 cups
2 cups canned or fresh, cooked (softened) chickpeas
Garam masala or black pepper for garnish

Procedure

1. In a heavy-bottomed skillet, heat oil over medium to low heat.

2. Fry the onion until very light golden brown. Add ½ cup water, bring to a boil, cover, and let simmer for 5 minutes. If the heat is too high, turn it to low.

3. To prepare masala, add salt, garlic, coriander, red pepper, cumin, turmeric, and tomatoes to the onion.

4. Cook for 5–10 minutes, stirring and scraping the bottom of the pan constantly. Continue until oil starts to separate from masala. Set aside.

5. Discard the liquid from the chickpeas and wash under running water.

6. Add chickpeas to the masala with ¼ cup of water. Stir, cover, and let simmer over low heat for 5–10 minutes

7. Transfer to a serving dish and garnish with garam masala or black pepper.

Breads

Plain Phulkas (Puffed Chapattis)

Plain Parathas

Stuffed Potato Parathas

Stuffed Mooli (Daikon Radish) Parathas

Naan

Try using organic whole wheat flour; if it is not available, you can add some bran to regular flour. Try using the dough hook on your standing mixer. It makes a great dough for flatbreads.

PLAIN PHULKAS (PUFFED CHAPATTIS)

Ingredients

2–2½ cups whole wheat flour, divided
1–1½ cups water
2 tablespoons butter, melted, or olive oil (optional)

Procedure

1. Place 2 cups flour in a broad, stainless steel pan or glass baking dish. Slowly mix a small amount of water into the flour. For excellent technique, knead with one hand while splashing water into dough with the other hand. Once the flour and water are mixed, knead with both hands until a soft and springy dough is formed. Let sit for 10 15 minutes.

   OR

   Use a food mixer with a dough hook on low speed. Once the flour and water are mixed, knead on high for 1 minute until a soft and springy dough is formed. The dough will pull away from the sides of the bowl and form a ball around the dough hook. Let sit for 10–15 minutes.

2. Divide the dough into 8 to 10 round balls (a bit smaller than golf-ball size).

3. Take one ball at a time and flatten it between your palms, forming a small cake.

4. Dust each side of the cake with extra flour. Then, flatten the cake using a rolling pin to about 6 to 8 inches across (should resemble a pancake). This is your rotti. (In Pakistan, a special wooden board, called a *chakla*, is used to perform this step. I use a Silpat and find it a better surface since I do not have to dust it with flour.)

5. When ready to make rottis, place a heavy-bottomed skillet (iron or nonstick) or *tawa* over medium heat, and let it get hot.

6. Gently pick up the rotti and place on the hot skillet or tawa.

7. Flip it quickly, within ½ minute, and cook the other side for1–2 minutes. (This process will help puff up the rotti.)

8. Cook both sides while lightly pressing the edges with a clean cotton dishcloth or paper towel. Rotti will turn a darker tan while it cooks. Remove from heat.

9. Keep the rotti warm in a heavy napkin or tortilla warmer.

10. Repeat steps 3-9 for the rest of the dough balls to make more rottis.

Tip: You may brush each rotti with a teaspoon of melted butter or olive oil. This will keep the rottis very soft until you are ready to eat.

PLAIN PARATHAS
These are like fresh flat croissants!

Ingredients
2 cups whole wheat flour, divided
½ teaspoon salt
½–1 cup water
½ cup vegetable oil

Procedure

1. Place 1½ cups flour and salt in a broad, shallow stainless steel pan or glass baking dish. Slowly mix a small amount of water into the flour. For excellent technique, knead with one hand while splashing water into the dough with the other hand. When flour and water are mixed, knead with both hands until a soft and springy dough is formed. Let sit for 10-15 minutes.

OR

   Use a food mixer with a dough hook on low speed. Once the flour and water are mixed, knead on high for 1 minute until a soft and springy dough is formed. The dough will pull away from the sides of the bowl and form a ball around the dough hook. Let sit for 10–15 minutes.

2. Divide the dough into 8 to 10 equal sized balls (about the size of a golf ball).

3. Taking one ball at a time, flatten it between your palms.

4. Dust each side of the cake with extra flour. Then, flatten using a rolling pin to about 6 to 8 inches across (should resemble a pancake). Perform this step on a Silpat or wooden cutting board.

For steps 5, 6 and 7, see photo on page 101

5. Spread 1 teaspoon of oil on the top side of the pancake. Roll cake into a snake (see diagram).

6. Coil snake upon itself so it looks like a snail shell (see diagram).

7. Place a heavy-bottomed skillet (iron or nonstick) or tawa over medium heat.

8. Lightly flour coiled ball on both sides. Place coiled ball on a floured surface (A cutting board or a Silpat). Using a rolling pin, flatten ball until it is about 8 to 10 inches across.

9. Use 2 tablespoons of oil to lightly grease the skillet. Pick up gently and transfer the flattened paratha to the hot skillet. As the paratha is cooking, spread 2–4 teaspoons oil on each side. Cook both sides until golden brown. While cooking, press edges of paratha with spatula. With practice, paratha will be evenly cooked and perfectly round.

10. Repeat steps 3 9 for rest of the dough balls to make the rest of the parathas.

11. Keep parathas in a pile in a heavy cloth till ready to serve.

STUFFED POTATO PARATHAS

Ingredients
3 medium-size potatoes
½ teaspoon ground red pepper
½ teaspoon ground cumin
½ teaspoon salt
2 cups whole wheat flour, divided
½–1 cup water
½ cup vegetable oil

Procedure
For Stuffing

1. Cut potatoes into half and boil in a medium-size pan in 2 cups of water. Remove from pan when fork tender. Cool until able to comfortably handle the potatoes. Mash the potatoes well.

2. Mix in spices and salt. Set aside.

For Dough

1. Place 1½ cups flour in a broad, shallow stainless steel or glass baking dish. Slowly mix a small amount of water into the flour. For excellent technique, knead with one hand while splashing water into dough with the other hand. Then knead with both hands until a soft and springy dough is formed. Let sit for 5 10 minutes.

OR

Place 1½ cups flour and ½ cup water in a food mixer with a dough hook on low speed. Add more water as needed. Once the flour and water are mixed, knead on high for 1 minute until a soft and springy dough is formed. The dough will pull away from the sides of the bowl and form a ball around the dough hook. Let sit for 10–15 minutes.

2. Divide the dough into 8 to 10 equal sized balls (about the size of a golf ball).

3. Taking one ball at a time, flatten it between your palms.

4. Dust each side of the cake with extra flour. Then, flatten using a rolling pin to about 6 to 8 inches across (should resemble a pancake). Use a wooden board or a Silpat to perform this step.

For steps 5, 6 and 7, see photo on page 101

5. Spread 1 teaspoon of oil on the top side of the cake. Spread 2 tablespoons of potato stuffing on the pancake.

6. Roll pancake into a snake, stuffing side tucked in (see diagram).

7. Place a heavy-bottomed skillet (iron or nonstick) or tawa over medium heat.

8. Coil snake upon itself so it looks like a snail shell (see diagram).

9. Lightly flour coiled ball on both sides. Place coiled ball on a floured board or use a Silpat. Using a rolling pin, flatten ball until it is about 8 to 10 inches across.

10. Pick up gently and transfer to slightly greased, hot skillet. As flatbread is cooking, spread 2–4 teaspoons oil on each side. Cook both sides until golden brown. While cooking, press edges of flatbread with spatula. With practice, flatbread will be evenly cooked and perfectly round.

11. Repeat steps 3-10 with the rest of the dough balls.

Tips: Best eaten warm. If stuffing is not well mashed, paratha will fall apart.

STUFFED MOOLI (DAIKON RADISH) PARATHAS

Makes about 8 servings

Ingredients

3 teaspoons salt
1 medium daikon radish, grated, about 2 cups
1 teaspoon cayenne pepper
2 teaspoons ground coriander
2 cups whole wheat flour, divided
½–1 cup water
½ cup vegetable oil

Procedure

For Stuffing

1. In bowl, sprinkle salt on grated radish and let sit 5 minutes. Rinse radish and squeeze out all water.
2. Place in small bowl and mix in cayenne and coriander. Set stuffing aside.

For Dough

1. Place 1½ cups flour in a broad, shallow stainless steel pan or glass baking dish. Slowly mix a small amount of water into the flour. For excellent technique, knead with one hand while splashing water into dough with the other hand. Knead dough with both hands at least 10 minutes (dough should appear moister than biscuit dough and should feel sticky, but not runny). Let sit for 10–15 minutes.
2. Pinch off a piece of dough and shape it into a ball (somewhat smaller than a golf ball). For proper technique, use both hands.
3. Place dough ball on well-floured surface. With rolling pin, flatten ball until it is the size and thickness of a small pancake.
4. Brush upper surface of pancake with 1 teaspoon oil.

Step 7

Step 6

Step 5

5. Spread thin layer of radish stuffing, about 2 tablespoons, on pancake.

6. Roll pancake into the form of snake, stuffing side inward.

7. Coil snake upon itself so it looks like a snail shell.

8. Lightly flour coiled ball on both sides. Place coiled ball on floured wooden board or Silpat. Using rolling pin, flatten ball until it is about the size of pita bread.

9. Place large skillet (preferably iron) over medium heat, and wait until it gets hot. Grease lightly.

10. Pick up paratha gently and transfer to the hot skillet. As flatbread is cooking, spread 2–4 teaspoons oil on each side. Cook both sides until golden brown. While cooking, press edges of flatbread with spatula. With practice, flatbread will be evenly cooked and perfectly round.

11. Repeat steps 3 10 with the rest of the dough balls.

Tips: If serving as appetizer, cut each bread into 8 wedge-shaped pieces. Serve alone or with plain yogurt that has been sweetened slightly with sugar. Serve soon after preparation. Wrap breads in clean cotton cloth to keep them warm and soft until ready to eat. To cut the spiciness or heat, use less red pepper.

NAAN

Ingredients
1 teaspoon sugar
1 package self-rising yeast
2 cups lukewarm water, separated
2 cups white flour
½ cup oil

Procedure

1. Add sugar and yeast to ½ cup water. Place flour in a broad, shallow, stainless steel baking dish. Add yeast and sugar mixture and oil to the flour. Adding a little water at a time, slowly knead the remaining water into the flour. Knead with both hands in the dish for at least 10 minutes. Dough should appear moister than biscuit dough and should feel sticky but not runny. You may also use a standing mixer with the dough-hook attachment for kneading. Keep dough in a warm place for 30–60 minutes.

2. Remove dough and knead on a well-floured surface for 5 minutes. You may also use a standing mixer with dough-hook attachment for kneading.

3. Place a heavy-bottomed, ovenproof skillet or tawa on medium heat and grease lightly. Turn oven to broil and adjust racks to 6–12 inches from upper heating element.

4. Take a small amount of dough and shape into a ball (about the size of a golf ball). Place on a well-floured surface. With a rolling pin, flatten the ball until it is the size and thickness of a small pancake, about 6 to 8 inches across. Pick up gently and transfer to hot skillet. Once one side is slightly cooked, flip the naan over and fully cook the other side.

5. Remove from skillet and place in the oven with the less-cooked side facing up. Broil for 2 to 4 minutes on high.

6. Repeat steps 3-5 till all the dough is used.

7. Wrap naan in a clean cotton cloth and keep warm and soft until ready to serve.

Tips: You can prepare a week's worth of naan at the same time and store in the freezer.

THE TANDOOR

As a young girl in Pakistan, I loved to sit and watch Ami Jan making rottis in the tandoor she had set up for hot weather in the back yard. Having our own tandoori oven was a big treat, something my clever mother had arranged to save time and feed her hungry kids.

Most tandoors were roadside stands, like the ones I would see sometimes when I was walking with my brothers. The men who ran them would get up early in the morning and set up to cook one simple curry, mostly dal or vegetable and tandoori rottis for the crowds of workers who would crowd around by lunchtime, a little like open-air, self-serve cafés.

The roadside tandoori ovens were big clay cylinders set into a raised wood platform. Inside the cylinder was a mud floor where the fuel for the fire would go. In Ami Jan's tandoor, she used wood and dried tree branches for fuel. Sometimes we kids would help out, stuffing the twigs down into the oven

The roadside tandoors were usually run by three people. The first person would prepare the dough for the bread, rolling it into small balls. The second person would take one dough ball at a time and flatten it into plate-size round flatbreads. He would put the flatbreads on a little pillow and stick his hand in the oven and plop the dough along its sides to cook. It was amazing, but he never burnt himself. After a few moments, the third person would use a three-feet-long hooked rod to remove the finished rottis and drop them to the side. The three people would work gracefully together for hours preparing rottis for the men who gathered at lunchtime.

Ami Jan did all three steps on her own, keeping the tawa over the opening until she was ready to cook. I loved to sit and watch her work.

The clouds of fresh bread scent smelled like heaven.

The clouds of fresh bread scent smelled like heaven. The finished ones went on changheris (decorated straw plates to hold the bread). I would get a cloth to wrap them, and then we would put them on a dining table until everyone was ready to eat. Mostly, we enjoyed the fresh baked bread with some kind of curry, meat or vegetable. On special occasions, Mom would stuff the dough with dal or potatoes before she cooked them. Or on summer nights, Ami Jan used gram flour to make parathas, which we followed with cold mangoes and lassi.

Rice

**Basmati Rice and
Peas Pilau**

**Basmati Rice and
Chicken Pilau***

**Basmati Rice with
Yellow Lentils (Kichari)***

You may substitute basmati rice with brown or any other kind of organic rice (the amount of water will vary whether you use brown rice or white rice). Do not hesitate to use your rice cooker! Remember to soak basmati rice for 10 minutes prior to cooking. Also, remember the ratio of water to rice is 2 to 1. I use all of the same recipes to cook other grain, like quinoa, to make a less starchy dish.

* Gluten free

BASMATI RICE AND PEAS PILAU*

Ingredients
½ small onion, chopped
¼ cup vegetable oil
½ teaspoon cumin seeds
2–4 cinnamon sticks, 2–4 inches long
1½ teaspoons salt
6 whole cloves
2 black cardamom seeds
2 teaspoons garlic powder or 3 garlic cloves, minced
4½ cups water, separated
2 cups basmati rice
1 cup frozen or fresh peas, sautéed in 2 tablespoons of oil or
   butter

Procedure
1. In a stainless steel, heavy-bottomed pan, sauté the chopped
    onions in vegetable oil until very dark brown. This will give a
    brownish color to the rice.
2. Add cumin seeds, cinnamon sticks, salt, cloves, cardamom,
    and garlic along with ½ cup of water.
3. Bring to a boil. Cover and let simmer on low heat for 5–7
    minutes.
4. While the above mixture is boiling, wash rice several times
    and soak for 5–7 minutes.
5. Add 4 cups of water to the pan from step 3 and bring to a
    boil.
6. Get rid of the soaking water and add the rice to the boiling
    mixture, stir, and cook, uncovered over medium heat until
    most of the water is evaporated.

7. Fluff the rice a few times using a fork while it is cooking.

8. When all of the water is evaporated, turn off the heat. Add the sautéed peas and mix gently. Cover and let sit for a few minutes. Serve with any kind of curry or yogurt.

BASMATI RICE AND CHICKEN PILAU*

Ingredients

½ small onion, chopped, about ½ cup

¼ cup vegetable oil

1 teaspoon cumin seeds

4 cinnamon sticks, 1–2 inches long

1 teaspoons salt

6 whole cloves

2 black cardamom seeds

2 teaspoons garlic powder or 3 garlic cloves, minced

1 pound chicken, dark meat, with or without bones, skin and fat
    removed

2 cups basmati rice

Procedure

1. In a stainless steel, heavy-bottomed pan, sauté the chopped
   onion in vegetable oil until very dark brown. This will give a
   brownish color to the rice.

2. Add cumin seeds, cinnamon sticks, salt, cloves, cardamom,
   garlic, and chicken. Cook on high to medium heat. Chicken
   will release water. Cook and stir, scrapping the bottom for
   about 10 minutes till the chicken turns brown and the water
   has evaporated.

3. Add 1 cup water. Bring to a boil. Cover and let simmer on
   low to medium heat for 10–15 minutes.

4. Wash rice several times and soak in 5 cups of water for 10
   minutes.

5. Remove the chicken from the broth. Remove the bones from
   the meat and cut it into 1- to 2-inch-thick pieces. Set aside.

6. Add 4 cups of water to the broth and bring to a boil.

7. Discard the water in which rice is being soaked and add only

the pre-soaked rice to the broth. Stir and cook, uncovered, over medium heat until most of the water is evaporated.

8. Fluff the rice a few times using a fork while it is cooking.

9. When all of the water is evaporated, turn off the heat. Add the cooked chicken pieces and mix gently. Cover and let sit for a few minutes.

10. Serve with any kind of curry or yogurt.

BASMATI RICE WITH YELLOW LENTILS (KICHARI)*

Makes 6 side servings

Ingredients

½ cup yellow dal (moong dal)
½ small onion, chopped
¼ cup vegetable oil
1–2 cinnamon sticks
5 cloves
2 black cardamom seeds
½ teaspoon cumin seeds
2 teaspoons garlic powder or 5 cloves garlic, crushed.
1–2 teaspoons salt
water
1 cup basmati rice

Procedure

1. Rinse dal several times in fresh water. Then, soak in fresh water for 10 minutes.

2. In a stainless steel saucepan, sauté chopped onion in oil until dark brown.

3. Add soaked yellow dal, all spices, salt, and 1½ cups water. Bring to a boil. Reduce heat to low. Cover and let simmer 20 minutes.

4. While dal simmers, rinse rice several times in fresh water. Then soak rice in fresh water for 10 minutes. After dal has simmered for 20 minutes, uncover saucepan and increase heat to medium. Stir frequently until thick mixture of dal in a small amount of liquid masala (spiced liquid) remains.

5. Add 2 cups water. Bring to a boil. Discard the water in which rice has been soaked and add only the rice to the pan. Stir and cook over medium heat. Fluff rice 3–4 times as water is evaporating. When all of the water has evaporated, turn heat to low. Cover and let sit 3–5 minutes. Turn heat off. Leave covered until ready to serve.

Tip: This is the most common comfort food in Pakistan. Serve with yogurt or any curry. Those who cook more delicately may tie the cinnamon sticks and cloves in cheesecloth and then retrieve them before serving.

Desserts

Ann's Favorite Sweet Potatoes*

Rice Kheer*

Swian (Vermicelli) and Egg Pudding

Ras Malai*

Lali's Semolina Halva

Gluten free

ANN'S FAVORITE SWEET POTATOES*

Ingredients

4 average-size sweet potatoes,
    scrubbed and washed thoroughly
4 tablespoons vegetable or olive oil
6 tablespoons brown sugar or 4 table-
    spoons maple syrup
½ teaspoon cinnamon

Lala's daughter Ann

Procedure

1. Slice the sweet potatoes in ¼-inch thick rounds.

2. In heavy-bottom skillet over medium to high heat, heat half of the oil and then spread half of the sweet potato slices in a single layer. Cook both sides until golden brown. Set aside.

3. Repeat step 2 with the second half of the sweet potatoes.

4. Place half of the sweet potatoes in an ovenproof, wide serving dish. Sprinkle with half the sugar or maple syrup. Add the rest of the potatoes and then the rest of the sugar or syrup. Sprinkle cinnamon on top.

5. Broil on high for 3–5 minutes. Let sit for 5 minutes. Serve.

Tip: Make sure that your sugar or maple syrup gets caramelized under the broiler.

RICE KHEER*

Ingredients
½ cup basmati or any rice
2 tablespoons oil or butter
¼ teaspoon crushed cardamom seeds
3 cups whole milk or 2 cups whole milk and 1 cup half and half
½ cup sugar
¼ cup slivered almonds
2 tablespoons yellow/dark raisins

Procedure
1. Cook rice according to the instructions on the package.
2. In a heavy-bottomed saucepan, heat oil or butter over medium heat. Add cardamom and cook 1 minute.
3. Add milk and bring to a boil.
4. Reduce heat to low and add rice and sugar.
5. Cook for 15–20 minutes on high to medium heat, stirring and scraping the bottom frequently. Kheer will start to thicken. Cook until it seems like a lumpy runny custard. Kheer will thicken more as it cools down.
6. Add almonds and raisins. Cook 2–3 minutes more.
7. Remove from heat and move kheer to serving dish.

Tip: Excellent food for babies who are just being introduced to solid foods.

SWIAN (VERMICELLI) AND EGG PUDDING

Ingredients
½ cup white or brown sugar
1 cup water
½ stick unsalted butter or ¼ cup vegetable oil
6 green cardamom seeds, semi-crushed
4 ounces Indian spaghetti, or *swian*, cut into 2- to 4-inch pieces
3 eggs, beaten

Procedure
1. Mix sugar and water, bring to a boil, and let simmer on low heat for 5–7 minutes.
2. In a heavy-bottomed skillet, melt butter or heat oil over low-medium heat.
3. Add cardamom seeds and swian, Keep on stirring and cooking swian over low-medium heat until golden brown. Flip swian often to brown evenly.
4. Add sugar syrup to the swian. Let cook for 5–7 minutes, stirring a few times, until most of the syrup is absorbed by the swian.
5. Lower heat and pour eggs over the swian. Do not stir. Cover and turn heat off and leave the skillet on the stove for 3–5 minutes.
6. Remove from stove. Mix gently with a fork and serve hot or cold.

Tip: Makes a good snack or a dessert with black tea or kava.

RAS MALAI*

Ingredients

2 pounds ricotta cheese

1 cup sugar, divided

2 eggs, well beaten

¼ teaspoon green cardamom seeds

2 quarts whole milk

8-ounce can evaporated milk or 1 cup half-and-half for a richer
   taste

¼ cup slivered pistachios or almonds

6 edible silver leaves (optional)

Procedure

For Ras Malai Dumplings

1. Mix cheese, ½ cup sugar, and beaten eggs thoroughly.

2. Bake in an 8″ x 8″ glass dish at 300° for 1 hour. This will
    make the ras malai pieces.

3. Remove pan from the oven and let cool at room
    temperature. Use a knife to cut into small pieces (1–2 inches)
    square. Set aside.

For Syrup

1. While above is baking, add ½ cup sugar and cardamom
    seeds to milk in a heavy-bottomed skillet. Bring to a boil on
    high heat.

2. As soon as the milk comes to a boil, reduce heat to low. Stir
    frequently, making sure to scrape the sides and the bottom
    of the pan. This process requires careful attention as milk
    burns easily. Keep on simmering until milk mixture is
    reduced to half its original volume.

3. Bring this condensed milk to room temperature and add 1 can of evaporated milk, or half-and-half, then mix, and refrigerate.

To Assemble Ras Malai

1. Mix the broken pieces and leftover scraps into the milk mixture.
2. Transfer the milk mixture to the serving dish and gently add ras malai pieces to the milk. Pieces break easily so be careful.
3. Let cool in a refrigerator for 3–24 hours.
4. Sprinkle with finely chopped pistachio or almond pieces and edible silver leaves before serving.

LALI'S SEMOLINA HALVA

Ingredients

¾ cups raw sugar, fructose crystals, or table sugar

1½ cups water

¼ cup vegetable oil or ½ stick unsalted butter

¼ teaspoon green cardamom seeds

1 cup course grain semolina flour (fine semolina makes halva taste like paste)

¼ cup raisins

¼ cup sliced almonds or pistachios

Procedure

1. In a small pan, add sugar to water. Bring to a boil and cook on medium heat until all of the sugar has dissolved. Leave solution on very low heat.

2. In a stainless steel frying pan, heat oil or butter over medium heat. Add cardamom seeds and cook for 30 seconds.

3. Turn the heat to low and add semolina. Keep on stirring the semolina and scrapping the bottom until it turns light brown and gives off a sweet smell (approximately 10–12 minutes). Remove from heat.

4. Stir sugar syrup into semolina. Place back on heat. Cook for 5–10 minutes, stirring frequently, until syrup is absorbed by the semolina and the halva is not runny but solid looking, like kneaded dough. Mix in raisins.

5. Transfer to a serving dish and sprinkle with sliced almonds or pistachios.

THE HALVA THAT KEPT ON GROWING

As the eldest daughter, I was occasionally asked to look after the younger children when my parents were out. Once when I was ten, I was asked to babysit my three younger brothers. As always, they were famished and eager to get into trouble. I decided to prepare some halva. A sweet treat, halva was sure to occupy the boys, fill their bottomless bellies, and make me their hero. Rehmat, our helper, was also there to encourage me to cook.

Halva is served as a simple dessert or as breakfast with fried flatbread. It is semolina that is browned in a little butter and then cooked with simple sugar syrup and combined with softened almonds. I had no idea of proportions, and to offer further distraction, the boys were clamoring around me, bouncing off the walls as little boys do.

"Oooooh, Appi [big sister] is using the fire!"

"You will get in trouble for using the angithee [stove], Appi."

"Do it, Appi! Pakau! Cook!" said Sikander.

"Yes, Appi! Do it! We won't tell Ami Jan! We'll say someone else did it!" said Tami.

They started chanting. "Halva! Halva! Halva!" I took four glasses of semolina (more than eight times the normal amount!) and almost as much clarified butter, or ghee. It smelled amazing as it fried, like sweet, citrus-infused butter. When I poured six glasses of sugar syrup on it, the halva swelled up like rice, puffing and puffing until it mushroomed up over the pan, spilling down the sides, burning my hand. I yanked my arm back as the boys stared in awe.

"Oooh, Lali made a never-ending halva!"

"It's spilling on the floor."

"Let's eat it anyway!"

And did we ever eat! I'll never forget the sight of my baby brother, Jimmy, licking his chubby little hands, or the sweet silence of little brothers happily gorging.

Drinks

SERVED COLD OR WITH ICE

Yogurt Lassi*

SERVED HOT

Green Tea and Cardamom Kava*

Chai*

Gluten free

YOGURT LASSI*
Served Cold or with Ice

Ingredients
1 cup plain yogurt (whole or low fat)
1 cup milk (whole or low fat)
3 tablespoons sugar or honey
$1/8$ teaspoon salt
Ice cubes

Procedure
In a blender, combine yogurt, milk, sugar or honey, salt, and ice cubes (start with about 8). Blend on high for 30 seconds to a minute. Pour into glasses; serve immediately.

Tip: Very refreshing on a hot summer day.

GREEN TEA AND CARDAMOM KAVA*
Served Hot

Ingredients
4 cups water, divided
2 bags green tea or 1 teaspoon loose green tea leaves
Pinch of baking soda
½ teaspoon green cardamom seeds, crushed
6 teaspoons sugar

Procedure
1. In a clean pan, boil 2 cups of water with tea, soda, and cardamom seeds. Cover and let simmer for 10 minutes over low heat.
2. Add remaining 4 cups cold water (this breaks the cell walls, releasing more color and flavor). Bring to a boil. Remove tea bags or leaves and discard. Lower the heat. Keep it on low heat until ready to serve.
3. Pour this kava into 4–6 individual cups. Add sugar to taste.

Tip: Great drink to serve with any dessert.

CHAI*
In Urdu, *chi* means simply "tea."

Ingredients
4 cinnamon sticks, 1–2 inches long, semi-crushed
1 clove
Seeds from 4 black or green cardamoms, crushed
4 cups water
4 bags black tea or 4 teaspoons loose black tea
1 cup whole milk
Sugar to taste
Salt to taste

Procedure
1. In a medium-size saucepan, add 2 cups of water, cinnamon sticks, clove, and cardamom seeds. Bring to a boil. Cover and let simmer for 10 minutes.
2. Add 2 more cups of water and the black tea to the simmering mixture. Bring it to a boil again.
3. Add milk to this tea mixture. Remove from heat and use a strainer to remove all solids from the tea.
4. Divide the prepared tea equally into 4 individual cups, add sugar and a pinch of salt in each cup.

Acknowledgments

The writing of this book has been a true labor of love for me. I could never have completed it without the generous assistance of my friends and family. I am grateful to:

— my daughters, for their ever-ready but always loving critique;

— my dear friend and ghostwriter who infused an inimitable appeal into my stories;

— Eli Simmonds for taking such fabulous food photos and always enjoying the food afterwards;

— Sheryn Hara and Julie Scandora for their encouragement and guidance;

— Laura Zugzda for her amazing talents that made my manuscript into a treat for the eyes;

— the producer of MasterChef USA for suggesting this title for my book;

— my amazing and beautiful mother. I love you, my Ami Jan.

Glossary

Abi Jan: Father dear

Aba Ji: Grandfather dear

amchoor: dried mango powder

Ami Jan: Mother dear

angithee: coal-filled stove

Appi: big sister

bahi: brother

bawarchi: a chef

besan: gram flour

Bi Ji: Grandmother dear

bili: female cat (the source for the author's nickname, Bilo, given by her grandparents)

bucha: child

chakla: small wooden board for rolling out dough to make bread

changheris: decorated tray to hold bread

chapatti: plain flatbread

chat: mixed cut fruit with spicy and sour sauce

chai: Urdu for tea

daikon radish: a large, elongated, white winter radish, used especially in Asian cuisine.

dal (also dahl): lentils

dupatta: scarf

garam: spicy, as in hot spicy

garam masala: a slightly hot mixture of various spices combined in a definite ratio, roasted, and ground to an aromatic mixture; mostly used as a garnish

ghee: clarified butter

gram: a kind of seed covered with black husk; used to make besan (gram flour)

halal: kosher

kaloniji: an herb used in pickling

kamiz: shirt

kava: tea with no milk or other ingredients added

khansama: a chef

kheer: rice pudding

kichari: rice with mong dal and certain whole spices

kofta: curried meatballs

kuchumar: beaten to a pulp; a kuchumar salad has very finely cut ingredients

Lali: nickname for Lala

lassi: cool yogurt drink

masala: "spice of life"; the heart of an excellent curry; the basic sauce

muchali walla: fish vendor

naan: yeasted flatbread

pakora: fried dumplings made of gram flour

Punjabi: Northwestern part of India and Pakistan

paratha: unleavened flatbread, cooked with oil, butter, or ghee

Phophoo: common name for fraternal aunt

phulka: puffed-up flatbread

rotti: type of flatbread

ryta: plain yogurt, mixed with chopped onions, cucumbers, and onions

saag: curried green leafy vegetables

seer: unit of measurement for weight, about 2 pounds

samosa: a triangular appetizer, filled with ground meat or potatoes and peas

shalwar: a type of trousers

swian: very thin noodles, also called vermicelli

tandoor: clay oven

tandoori rotti: flatbread baked in clay oven (tandoor)

tawa: circular hot plate to cook chapattis

Index

kuchumar salad, 58

lady fingers, 77
Lala
    cooking philosophy, x
    culinary history, vii-viii
    and friend Kitto, 39–40
    photos, vi, 17, 41, 59
lamb curry, 32–33
lassi, 105. *See also* yogurt
lemon pickle, 24
lentils, 83
    with basmati rice, 112
lettuce. *See* salad
limes, 24

maash dal, 84, 85
mango, 14
    chutney, 21, 23
    memories of, vii, 15–16, 80
    pickling marathon, 25–27
    powder, 2, 10, 11, 13
masala, 31, 32
    koftas (meatballs) and, 34, 35
    fish curry and, 44
    meat curry and, 32
    shrimp curry and, 46
    vegetable, 67, 72–73, 76–77, 78–79
masoor dal, 84, 85
meatballs, 34–35
meat dishes, 29
mint, 2, 14
    chutney, 9, 22, 49, 50
    as garnish, 20, 21, 57, 58, 64, 78–79

shrimp
    curry, 46
    kabobs, 14
spices, ix
    ground, 1
    whole, 1
spinach pakoras, 6
spinach saag, 74–75
split peas, 83
squash curry, 72–73
sweet-and-sour dressing, 12
sweet potatoes, 116
swian and egg pudding, 118

tamarind, 2, 13
    chutney, vii, 2, 8–9, 10, 14, 20, 50
tandoori bread and ovens, 43, 104
tea. *See* chai
tilapia, 48
tomatoes with potatoes ryta, 56
turmeric, 1

vegetable curries, 67, 78
vegetable oil, ix
vegetable vendors, 80–81
vegetarian dishes, x
    haleem, 88–89
vermicelli and egg pudding, 118

wraps, stuffing for, 7

yogurt (lassi), vii, 105, 125, 126. *See also* rytas
    with rice, 109, 111, 113

zucchini curry, 71–72